How to COOK Your CATCH!

By JEAN CHALLENGER

Illustrations by NELSON DEWEY

Cover photo courtesy Fisheries Council of B.C.

Jean Challenger was born and raised in Prince Rupert, B.C. She was married in 1946 and moved to Vancouver to live. Since 1958 the Challengers have had a summer home on Thetis Island in the Gulf Islands. They had a twenty foot boat for three years before that. This is where Jean has learned about the different shellfish and fish on the B.C. coast and where she has developed the recipes in this book.

Here's a book written for fishermen and beachcombers who'd like to cook their catch on board a boat .... or at a cabin or cottage — wherever many of the "modern conveniences" are missing!

The recipes and cooking methods in this book are especially created for use with a minimum amount of simple utensils and equipment — and a maximum of convenience and eating pleasure!

How to Cook Your Catch contains many recipes — for all types of fish, crabs, shrimp, clams, oysters, abalone, limpets!

Special section on preparing exotic seafoods like sea cucumber, seaweed, moon snails, chitons, sea urchins!

How to prepare sauces, pastries and other complementary dishes!

Also — Clear, easy to follow directions on how to clean the various fish and sea life!

PUBLISHED BY
HERITAGE HOUSE PUBLISHING COMPANY LTD.
Box 1228, Station A, Surrey, B.C. V3S 2B3

PRINTING HISTORY
First printing 1973; second, 1974; third, 1975; fourth, 1977; fifth, 1979; sixth, 1981; seventh, 1986; eighth, 1990.

Canadian Cataloguing in Publication Data
Challenger, Jean.
 How to cook your catch!

 Originally published: Sidney, B.C.: Saltaire Pub., 1973 ISBN 0-88792-017-9 pa.

 1. Cookery (Fish). 2. Cookery (Seafood).
 I. Title
 TX 747.C44 1977 641,6'92 C77-002089-5

Printed in Canada

ACKNOWLEDGMENTS

My thanks to my husband, children and daughter-in-law for sampling my recipes and giving me ideas. Also thanks to the girls in my bridge club for their suggestions. Thanks to my American friend, Eli, for Seasoned Spinach; to my Hawaiian friend, Barbara, for Pickled Japanese Seaweed; to Peggy from Nova Scotia for Crowfoot Greens; and to Norm from Thetis Island for Smoked Salmon and How to Make a Salmon Smoker. Thanks to B.C. Packers Home Economist, Jan, for her help. Thanks also to Charlie and Nelson for helping me to write my first book.

Hope you enjoy cooking your catch as much as I have enjoyed working out the recipes for you.

Jean Challenger

CONTENTS

Steelhead or Trout .... Salmon Scalloped Fish .... Salmon Loaf .... Salmon with Celery Soup .... Creamed Onion Fish .... Salmon Souffle .... Bouillabaisse .... Make a Salmon Smoker .... How to Smoke Salmon.

INTRODUCTION

I have written these recipes so that you can start from the beginning, step by step, getting things out as you need them. There isn't too much counter space aboard boats so it is easier to do it this way. The **ingredients** in each recipe are set in **Boldface type** so you can see at a glance what you will need.

Recipes marked with two asterisks (**) can be cooked on top of the stove as well as in an oven. I prefer to finish them off in the oven as they look more appetizing and they can also be served piping hot. However, when you are outdoors camping or boating, any food looks good.

I've also kept in mind that there will be men trying these recipes. My 19 year old son, Jim, can follow them, so...good luck fellows!

Following are some cooking tips to use when camping or boating—and a list of basic cooking equipment for use on a boat or in a camp...

9

I suggest using a double boiler in many of my recipes. I have found through the years that with four children to keep track of, and other interruptions, food is forever getting burned, especially anything with milk in it. It is such a waste of time scrubbing burn off pots!

A *double boiler* allows you to cook without burning- -and it also keeps food hot until you are ready to eat. (Use the hot water from the bottom of the boiler for washing up.) A make-shift double boiler can be made by nesting a smaller pot in a larger pot or frypan with a jam lid under the small pot to keep it off the bottom. You have to watch that the water doesn't boil away if using this arrangement!

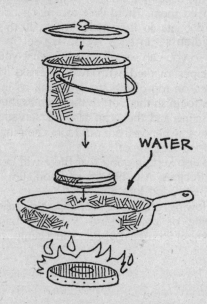

WATER

Never use pepper or any strong sauce with sea food. If anyone insists, let them add it themselves as they eat it! The marvelous flavour of shrimp, crab, clams, cod, salmon, etc., is bland and subtle, and will be drowned if strong spices or sauces are used.

You will find in my recipes that I call for green onions. They add a little color to food and therefore make it more appetizing. However, if you are where you can't get green onions, cooking onions can be substituted.

You can substitute pre-cooked rice for uncooked. I think the uncooked rice has a nicer taste, and you must remember the uncooked rice triples in volume when cooked and the pre-cooked rice doesn't quite double. (This will affect the amount in each serving.) A tablespoon of vegetable oil in the water in which you are cooking the rice will calm the water down so it is not so apt to boil over.

My husband dislikes parsley so I use green pepper You use the one you and your husband like.

If using frozen fish, be sure to cook it before it completely thaws. It then has a flavor like fresh fish.

Left-over egg whites can be used as a fishdip before coating it in cracker or bread crumbs.

If you are on a boat or camping, cover your cooking pan with foil *before* you put in the fish as this saves a lot of washing, scrubbing and water.

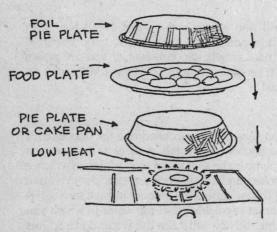

FOIL PIE PLATE →

FOOD PLATE →

PIE PLATE OR CAKE PAN →

LOW HEAT →

On small boats you are limited to doing your cooking on a small 2 burner Coleman, propane or alcohol stove. Keeping food hot until ready to serve is a problem we solved by putting a pie plate or cake pan upside down over the element! Set your plate of food on this and cover the food with a foil pie plate. Turn the heat down very low!

If you do not have a rolling pin use a glass jam jar on a piece of waxed paper to make the bread or cracker crumbs.

When fishing from a boat, have a pail, tub, or fish box to keep your fish fresh ... and to eliminate the mess of scales, slime, blood in your cockpit.

COVER FISH WITH DAMP CLOTH (BURLAP, ETC.), KEEP OUT OF SUN!

When cleaning fish at camp I work on newspaper and put the cleanings in a pail. Take the cleanings down to the water and feed the seagulls: (Or save them for your crab or shrimp traps. See Heritage House Books *How to Catch Crabs!* and *How to Catch Shellfish!*) If the gulls don't get it the crabs, starfish and dogfish will. Burn the newspaper or put it with your garbage.

Be sure and wash up the area where you have been cleaning fish or shellfish. Otherwise you will have a dreadful smell and problems with insects, mink, rodents, crows, etc.

Keep salt by putting rice in the shaker and sealing with Saran or plastic wrap when you won't be aboard the boat for any long periods. There are plastic salt and pepper shakers that have tops that seal out moisture—useful for anywhere around water.

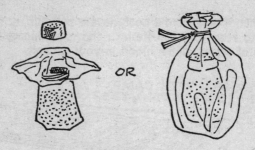

OR

I keep my bag of flour and bag of sugar in medium sized plastic garbage bags sealed with their wire ties. When you are away from your boat during wet weather put your spices in plastic bags. The same applies to anything that gets damp like crackers, cereal, etc.

An iron frying pan is ideal, but it is heavy and will rust if not well oiled and sealed in a plastic bag. Thinner frypans are inclined to burn food in the middle, but if you are packing on your back you have to use this kind. The food must be kept moving around in the pan to get things to brown evenly. (Bacon strips must be cut in three pieces — otherwise the centre is cooked and the two sides are half cooked!)

Always drain your fried food on paper towelling as this improves the flavour and texture.

Please keep our beaches and waters clean! Dispose of what you can't safely burn--paper plates, plastic bags, bottles and cans—at a Marina or by taking them home and disposing of them there! The gulls will eat food scraps and fish cleanings, but whatever you do, *don't* leave fish cleanings on shore for the mink, otter or racoons! They will take it into their den under the rocks or into holes and *wow* the smell! However, if you or a neighbor have a cat, save the fish heart and liver, as they just love them.

If you don't get around to filleting your fish right away clean it, wrap it in newspaper and lay it flat in the refrigerator. (It is very difficult to fillet a "U" shaped fish!)

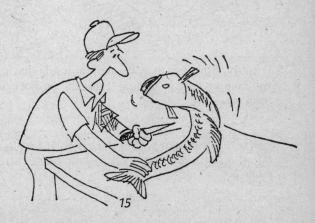

For campfire cooking take along a rack from an old stove oven. Place it on rocks with the hot coals under it. Pots will get black. The worst of this can be cleaned off with sand from the beach. Applying soap (liquid, or powdered mixed with water) to the sides and bottom (outside!) *before* cooking may make the cleanup easier! Again, plastic bags in which to keep each pot save you having to clean soot off other utensils.

Rubbing lemon juice on your fingers will help keep fish odors from clinging to them.

You can use chicken wire to make an envelope to hold fish when barbecuing. *Be sure to oil it well!* It doesn't get too hot so is fairly easy to turn.

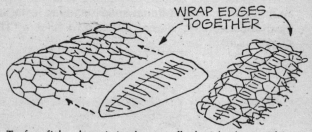

WRAP EDGES TOGETHER

To fry fish, place it in the pan flesh side down. This will help prevent its curling. Have the fat hot but not smoking.

A wire brush from a paint store is great for cleaning off your barbecue grill. Watch your fingers so they don't get jabbed.

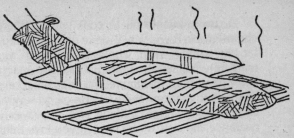

I have also used two flat aluminum cookie sheets to turn large fillets of salmon. This was the top two-thirds of a thirty pound salmon. It worked like a charm.

Keep all left-over cooked fish, flake it from any bones and skin, and use it in chowders, casseroles, salads, etc. Also use where a recipe calls for canned fish.

To store in a refrigerator, wipe fish with a damp cloth and keep it in a tightly closed container — in the coldest part of the refrigerator.

Before frying fish, make sure you have dried it thoroughly, to prevent the fat splattering.

From the time you light charcoal briquets, it takes anywhere from 30 to 45 minutes, depending on the draft, before they will be ready. If your cottage (or Marina) has electricity available, the electric starting loop is great to start a barbecue. It is quick and clean, no smell and no flames shooting up. A pair of hinged spoons or sterilizing tongs are great for moving your briquets into place. Wear cooking mitts on your hands.

I use vegetable oil to cook with as there is no cholesterol in it and very little in fish. Any hard animal fat is *loaded* with cholesterol. Hard vegetable margarine has less than animal fat. Soft margarine is better than hard margarine. Oil does have calories so be sure and drain anything fried in oil on several layers of paper towelling. Draining also improves the appearance and taste of the food. If you love things fried in butter, use oil and flavor it with a small spoonfull of butter.

All fats and oils have about nine calories per gram [270 per ounce]. The use of saturated fats — butter, meat fats, coconut oil — should be restricted as it can cause the body to produce chloresterol.

When a recipe calls for "grated Cheddar cheese with skim milk powder" I am referring to the Kraft brand packaged as a mixture of both.

Bouillabaisse - "Boo-Ya-Bess"- a chowder made of two or more kinds of fish and sometimes seasoned with wine.

Chowder - a dish consisting of fresh fish, clams, etc. stewed with vegetables, often in milk.

Saute' - "So-Tay" - fried quickly and turned frequently in a little oil.

Sauterne - "So-Turn" - a white table wine.

Tbsp - level tablespoon measure

Tsp - level teaspoon measure

Mousse - "Moose" - a light, frothy or foaming dessert or topping

Hors d'oeuvres - "Or Durvs" - appetizers.

SUGGESTED BASIC COOKING EQUIPMENT

1 large iron frying pan
1 medium size double boiler
1 large preserving kettle for cooking crabs, clams, etc.
1 or 2 egg lifters (spatula) for turning fish, etc.
1 pair of sterilizing tongs or hinged spoons for picking
   up hot racks, crabs, etc.
1 long handled cooking fork
Butcher knife
Oyster knife

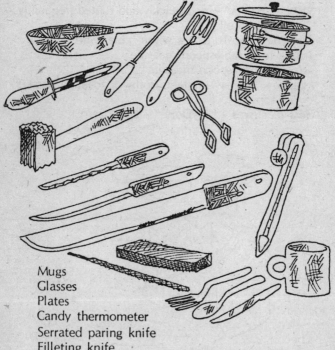

Mugs
Glasses
Plates
Candy thermometer
Serrated paring knife
Filleting knife
Whetstone for sharpening knives
Wooden mallet or piece of 2x4 for pounding abalone,
   limpets, etc.

Knives, forks and small and large spoons
Foil pie plates for keeping food hot
Skewers
Set of bowls
Lemon Juice (or "ReaLemon")
Heavy aluminum pie plate or cake pan for keeping
  food hot
Dishpan
Plastic pail for gathering oysters, clams, etc.

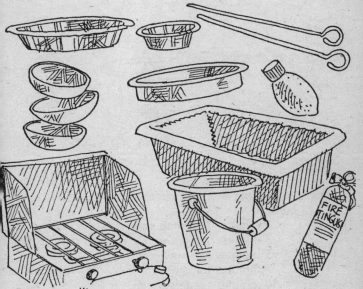

Paper towelling
Roll of garbage bags, large baggies and small baggies.
Roll of heavy aluminum foil
Saran wrap or any transparent plastic wrap
Stove - Coleman, propane, alcohol, oil, small hibachi,
  barbecue, etc.
Oven attachment for stove
Fire Extinguisher!

21

COOKING TIMES FOR SHELLFISH

Cook by dropping into a pot of boiling sea water. You can use salted fresh water but the flavour is not as good. The time depends on the size of the shell fish.

From the time the sea water *returns to the boil:*

      2 minutes for small shrimp
      3 minutes for prawns or cleaned crab pieces
      5 minutes for small crab
      7 minutes for medium crab
    10 minutes for large crab
    10 minutes for small lobster
    12 minutes for medium lobster
    15 minutes for large lobster

Scampi and crayfish will be the same as shrimp and prawns depending on the size.

Accurate timing on the barbecue is absolutely impossible because of the following variables:

1. Temperature of food when it starts cooking.
2. Temperature of fire.
3. When outdoors the temperature of the atmosphere and the prevailing winds.

Chart of approximate timings of seafood.
To test fish for doneness, use a fork. If it flakes easily and had lost its translucent look, it is done.
Fish Steaks, fillets and whole fish

Thickness	Time
1 inch	6 - 9 mins.
1-1/2 inches	8 - 12 mins.
2 inches	10 - 18 mins.

No need to turn thin steaks; turn midway for thick ones. Brush well with oil and lemon.

If the fish is more than 2 inches thick, fillet it. The larger fish dry out on the outside before the inside is cooked.

BAKED FISH TIMING

Bake at 450 degrees for approximately ten minutes for each inch of thickness. If wrapped in foil, 15 minutes for each inch of thickness. If hard frozen, 20 minutes for each inch of thickness.

HOW TO REMOVE SALT FROM SALTED FISH

Cut fish into small pieces and soak in ample water for two to four hours in fridge. Drain. Replace with **half milk** and **half water** plus **one tsp of white sugar**. Soak fish in fridge eight to ten hours. Drain and blot dry with paper towelling. It's now ready to use but don't add salt without tasting it first!

Sauces, Toppings, Etc.

HOLLANDAISE SAUCE FOR FISH, CRAB, SHRIMP, ETC.

Have the **fish prepared and hot,** ready for the sauce to be poured on and served immediately, as the butter separates in the sauce if left standing.

Put the bottom of a double boiler on the stove and keep the water hot--not boiling.

Have the **sherry** at hand if you are going to use it.

Have the kettle boiling as you will need a small amount of **boiling water.**

With the top of the double boiler on the counter mash **1/4 lb.** of **butter** from fridge until soft and creamy — do not melt.

Drop in **three egg yolks,** one at a time, and beat with a fork until creamy. (Keep the whites as they can be used in the Fish Souffle.)

Add **1 tbsp of lemon juice** (or Realemon, etc.),

A **dash of cayenne,**

Add **1/4 tsp of salt.** Beat well with a fork.

Cook over hot (not boiling) water, stirring continuously until mixture **thickens slightly.**

*(See note below.)

Adjust heat so that water simmers.

Slowly add **1/4 cup of boiling water** and **2 tbsps of medium-dry cocktail sherry** (or 1/3 cup of boiling water if you're not using the sherry).

Stir continuously until the mixture is like custard.

Serve immediately over seafood.

I've had the Hollandaise Sauce served over crab as an appetizer at a fancy restaurant. It was served in an oyster shell with the sauce poured over the seafood. A sprinkle of powdered grated cheddar cheese was on top. It had been popped into a 450 degree oven for two minutes so it was piping hot. It was delicious. This sauce can be served over crab, shrimp, flaked cod, flaked salmon, etc. as an appetizer or as an entree.

*

(If you are not going to serve this sauce immediately, remove it from the heat after "....until mixture **thickens slightly**.", and set it aside. Then, five minutes before serving, place it over simmering water and continue recipe at "Adjust heat....".

HOLLANDAISE MOUSSE

For those who like to live it up.
Fold **2 parts of Hollandaise Sauce** that has cooled into
1 part whipped cream and serve immediately over
cold seafood cocktail.

LEMON FISH MARINADE

Use **lemon juice** with a little **salt** added and let the fish fillets or steaks sit in this for at least 1 hour. Drain and blot dry before cooking.

SOYA SAUCE MARINADE

Combine equal parts of **soya sauce, medium dry Sauterne** and **vegetable oil.** Let the fish sit in this for at least 1 hour. Drain and blot dry before cooking. Soya sauce is very salty so taste before you add salt when cooking.

Mix and match, some or all. Your choice!

**Cubes of salmon, cod or any white fish,
Scallops, shrimp, oysters, chunks of lobster.**

**Mushrooms, cherry tomatoes, red and green
pepper squares.**

Pineapple chunks, olives, bacon rolls.

Oil the skewers and alternate your choice of
seafoods and vegetables, etc. Use the Soya Sauce
Marinade or Lemon Fish Marinade - see recipes.
Cook over barbecue or hibachi (not long) until
done .

CHEESE BISCUITS

3 cups all purpose pre-sifted flour
6 tsp Magic baking powder
3/4 tsp salt
1/4 cup butter or margarine, chilled
1 cup grated Canadian cheddar cheese (strong, do not pack)
1 cup of milk (1-1/2 for drop biscuits)

Mix first four ingredients until finely crumbled. Add grated cheese and mix slightly. Add milk to make a soft dough that can be cut into biscuits or add extra milk and drop by the tablespoon on a greased cookie sheet or into greased small tart pans. Bake at 450 degrees about 8 minutes for small biscuits.

If you do not have cheese and want to make plain biscuits increase the butter or margarine to 1/2 cup. These cheese biscuits make an appetizing snack by themselves or to complement another dish such as crab salad.

These can be dropped from a tablespoon onto a lightly oiled frypan (medium heat -- about 350°) with the lid on. Cook about six minutes each side.

Before I ate spinach cooked in this manner, my opinion of it was: "ugh!!" My children and friends love it cooked this way.

Put into a large bowl:
1/2 envelope of onion soup mix, and 1 tsp of flour. Mix.

Pour in **half of a 10-oz. carton of sour cream** and mix well.

Cut up a **10-oz. package of washed fresh spinach,** well drained.
Put the cut up spinach into the sour cream mix and keep folding until it is very well mixed and packs.

Cover a cookie sheet with foil and butter the foil. Spread the spinach mix on the sheet of buttered foil.

Dot with thin **slivers of butter** and

Sprinkle with **grated parmesan cheese.**

Bake at 350 degrees for approximately 20 minutes.

If the spinach is fresh and you have to wash it, dry it by draining well and by blotting it with paper towelling. You may have to increase the flour slightly to take care of the extra water.

This amount serves 4 people.

CHEESE CRACKER TOPPING FOR CASSEROLES

Roll into fine crumbs **20 unsalted crackers** on a
sheet of waxed paper with a rolling pin or jam jar.
Add 1/4 cup of grated cheddar cheese with skim
milk powder and mix well.
Pour into a 9 oz. jam jar and use as needed for
topping casseroles.
This may be prepared ahead of time and kept
refrigerated. Or, it will stay fresh for a few days
out of the fridge.

MOCK TARTAR SAUCE

If you don't have tartar sauce on hand mix up the
following--it makes a great substitute!
1/2 cup of mayonnaise and
Stir in **1 tbsp of prepared hot dog relish.** (Nalley's
or Bicks for example.)

BOTTOMFISH
Cod, Sole, Perch, Snapper, Rockfish, Flounder or any Mild White Fish.

HOW TO COOK BOTTOM FISH

These fish are delicious and mild flavored. When filleted they have very little bone. If cooked in several different ways you can have the white fish three or four times a week and never tire of it. The secret to cooking fish is to cook it fresh and <u>if it has been frozen then cook it before it completely thaws.</u>

How to clean and fillet Bottomfish

IN FILLETING FISH, THE OBJECT IS TO SEPARATE THE SKIN -- AND THE BONES, INTERNAL ORGANS AND HEAD--FROM THE MEAT (FILLETS)....

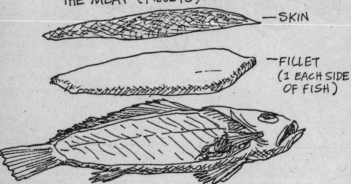

—SKIN

—FILLET (1 EACH SIDE OF FISH)

...THIS IS ACCOMPLISHED BY ANY OF SEVERAL METHODS...

WE'VE OBSERVED PROFESSIONALS CLEANING AND FILLETING FISH, AND THEIR METHODS (SHOWN HERE) SEEM TO BE THE FASTEST AND EASIEST.

(A) Make first cut behind gills and fin. Cut down to backbone, then parallel to it, almost to the tail

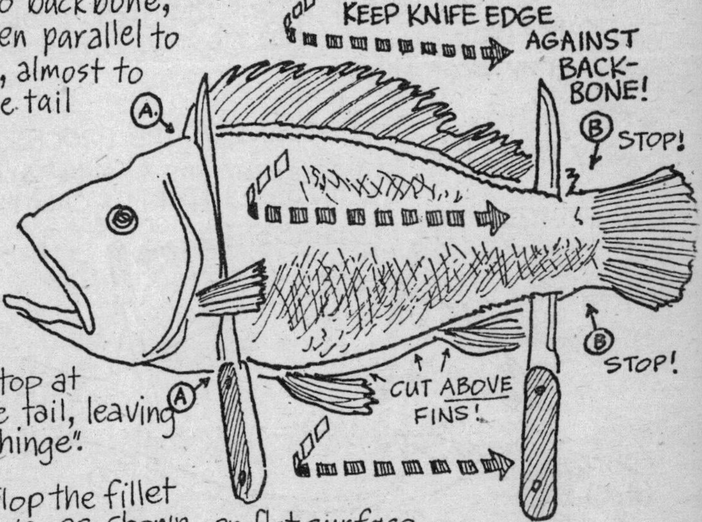

KEEP KNIFE EDGE AGAINST BACKBONE!

(A)

(B) STOP!

CUT ABOVE FINS!

(B) STOP!

Stop at the tail, leaving a "hinge".

(A)

Flop the fillet over as shown, on flat surface, still attached at the tail "hinge".

(FILLET)

(D)

(D) Continue cutting, with edge pressed against skin, to remove fillet from the skin.

... Then turn fish over and repeat process on the other side...

35

CONTINUED →

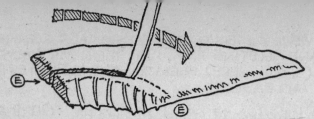

Ⓔ When you've separated the fillets from the skin... cut out the ribcage bones from each fillet.

● FOR _FLAT FISH_ (SOLE, FLOUNDER) THE PROCESS IS VERY SIMILAR... (Large specimens & halibut are usually gutted & cut into chunks or steaks.)

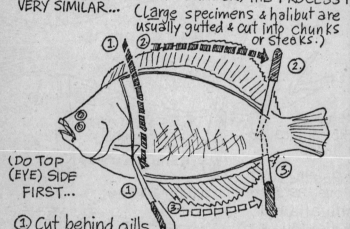

(DO TOP (EYE) SIDE FIRST...

① Cut behind gills & fin to depth of backbone.

② Start at first cut, and cut parallel to back-bone... almost to the tail.

③ Make cut from other end of first cut, towards tail to cut loose any part of the fillet you didn't get on #2 cut. Go almost to tail, then flop fillet... cut it from the skin and then do the other side of the fish in the same way.

36

Wash fillets in cold water. Drain and blot dry with paper towelling. Wrap and separate the fillets with plastic wrap so they will be easy to get apart. Now wrap the covered fillets in foil or freezer wrap. Label and date. Use before **2 months** at most.

If I have several rockfish to do I take the tin snips and cut off the sharp spines so I don't get jabbed. Be sure to clean them off when you are finished. Never ignore a jab, cut or scratch from around the seashore as it can become infected very easily. Wash it well and put a disinfectant on right away!

RAW COD HORS d'OEUVRES (or any mild white fish)

The Hawaiians love this treat.

Use only **fresh caught fish.**

Slice the raw filleted fish into **thin** wafers.

Arrange on a plate of **chopped lettuce.**

In a custard cup mix **1/2 tsp of hot mustard** with a little **water.**

Add **1/2 cup of soya sauce** and stir well.

Place this in the center of the plate.

Dip the raw fish in the sauce with a toothpick and serve with small crackers.

FISH CHOWDER

(Any mild white fish can be used like cod, sole, flounder, ling cod, halibut, red snapper, rockfish, etc.)

Put the bottom of the double boiler on to **simmer** as you will need it in a few minutes to keep the chowder hot.

Dice **1 medium onion** (approximately 1 cup) and

Dice **1 medium potato.**

Cut the **fish** into small pieces [**Approximately 1 cup**].

Cut **2 slices of side bacon** into small pieces.

Fry bacon in top half of double boiler at medium heat. (Not on bottom half of boiler!)

Pour off excess fat.

Add fish and fry for 1 minute.

Add onion and fry for another minute.

Add **1 cup of water,**

Add potato and let simmer until vegetables are cooked.

Place pot in the top of the double boiler and Add **2 cups of milk or cream,**

Add **1/4 to 1/2 tsp of salt** to taste.

Serve when hot. Do not boil.

This fish chowder can be varied by adding a tin of **tomato soup** to it.
This amount makes a generous serving for six.

FRIED COD (or any mild white fish)

In a small bowl whip **1 egg** with a fork,

Add a **dash of salt.**

In another bowl put **dried bread or cracker crumbs.**

Cut the **cod** into pieces,

Dip each piece in the egg and then in the crumbs.

Fry at a low to medium heat in vegetable oil until golden brown.

Sprinkle a **dash of salt** on each side as it fries.

Drain on paper towelling.

The pieces of cod may be deep fried.

BAKED COD (or any mild white fish)

Rub fillets with **lemon juice.**

Place fillets on an **oiled pan.**

Sprinkle with **salt** and your favorite seasoning.

Bake at 450 degrees for approximately 10 minutes for each inch of thickness.
(Bake for 15 minutes for each inch of thickness if the fish is wrapped in foil or for 20 minutes for each inch of thickness if the fish is hard frozen.)
Serve with tartar sauce or ketchup.

CREAMED COD (or any mild white fish)

Simmer the fish — about 1 cup (1/2 lb.) — in salted water until cooked.

Drain and cool.

In a double boiler make a medium white sauce as follows:

Melt **2 tbsp of margarine or butter.**

Add **2 tbsp of flour,**

1/2 tsp of salt and mix.

Pour in **1 cup of milk or cream** and stir continuously until thick.

Add flaked fish and
1 hard boiled egg diced.

Season to taste.
Serve over toast or rice.

COD TURNOVER FILLING (or any mild white fish)

Chop finely **1 cup of cooked cod** and **1 hard boiled egg** together in a bowl.

Watch for and pick out small bones!

In the top of a double boiler on the counter Stir **1 tsp of corn starch** into **1/2 cup of milk.**

Now put the complete double boiler over the heat. Stir continuously until thickened.

(If you have to haul Junior out of the saltchuck or chase a raccoon out of camp before it is thick, take it off the heat and set it in a cool place. I once ended up with a lumpy mess when I forgot to do this and had to throw it out and start over again).

Turn the heat under the double boiler to simmer.

Beat in cod and egg,

Add **1 tbsp of hot dog relish,**

1 tbsp of ketchup,

2 tbsp of mayonnaise,

1 tbsp of margarine or butter,

A **dash of salt,**

A **dash of nutmeg,** stir well and then set to cool. This is enough filling for 16 - 4" circles of pastry.

COD TURNOVER PASTRY

In a bowl place **2-1/4 cups of pre-sifted flour.**
(Use it right out of the bag, do not re-sift).

Add **1 tsp of salt, 1/2 tsp of thyme, 1/2 tsp of garlic salt, 2 tbsp of grated cheddar cheese with skim milk powder.**

Put **3/4 cup of hard margarine** in a bowl with the flour and cut it into small pieces.

Take off your rings, clean your nails, scrub your hands and then crumble the mixture with your finger tips.
Cut in **1/2 cup of cold water** and then blend with your fingers.

Roll out the pastry to an 1/8 thickness and cut out circles with a large can or saucer.
Wet the edges of each circle of pastry with cold water so they will seal together when cooked.
Put a spoonfull of Cod Turnover Filling on half of the circle of pastry.

Fold the pastry over the filling and seal the edges.

(continued on next page)

COD TURNOVERS
(continued from previous page)

Cover a cookie sheet with foil.
Do not butter it.

Place the turnovers on the foil.
Prick the top of each turnover twice with a fork to
let the steam out. (If you forget to do this and you
did a good job of sealing the edges the turnovers
could pop.)

Bake in a 350 degrees oven for 20 to 25 minutes
until golden brown.

Use the left-over pastry as a crust for a fish or
chicken casserole or it can be frozen after sealing
it in a plastic sandwich bag.

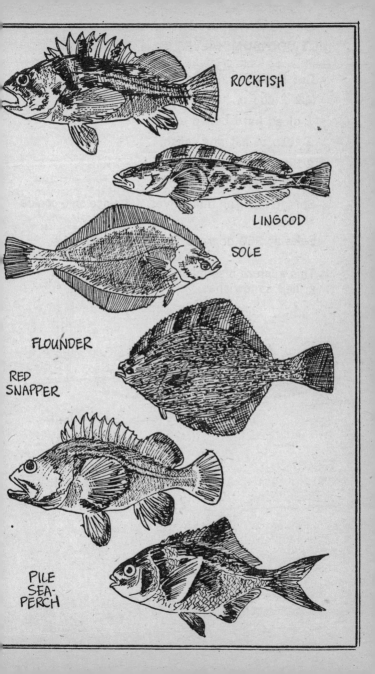

ROCKFISH

LINGCOD

SOLE

FLOUNDER

RED
SNAPPER

PILE
SEA-
PERCH

HOT COD BUN HALVES (Or any white fish)

Cut **buns** in half and butter them.

Mix **1 cup of flaked cooked cod** with

1 diced hard boiled egg,

1 tbsp of hot dog relish,

2 tbsp of mayonnaise and a
Dash of salt and mix well.

Spread filling on bun halves and place on a cookie
sheet.

Bake at 350 degrees for 10 minutes.

This mixture also makes a nice filling for plain or
grilled sandwiches.

COD WITH MUSHROOM SOUP(or ány mild white fish) **

Cut up **1 lb. of cod** (approximately 2 cups) into pieces and place in the bottom of a buttered casserole.

In a bowl put:
1 can of Cream of Mushroom soup (10 oz.)

1/4 cup of milk.

1/4 cup of soft cheese spread (e.g., "Cheez-Whiz")

1 tbsp of chopped green onion.

Mix the above ingredients well and pour over the fish in the casserole.

Sprinkle the top with **grated cheddar cheese or paprika.**

Bake at 350 degrees for 30 - 35 minutes approximately.

For a change crumble 2 slices of crisply cooked bacon and add instead of cheese spread.

** This recipe can be cooked in a double boiler on simmer if you are on a boat and don't have an oven.

FISH SOUFFLE (Cod or any white fish)

In (the top of) a double boiler melt:
2 tbsp of butter.

Add 2 tbsp of flour,

Dash of nutmeg or curry

1/2 tsp of salt.

Stir in 3/4 cup of milk and stir constantly until thick.

Remove from stove and stir in
1/4 cup dried bread or cracker crumbs and
1 cup of cooked flaked fish.

Separate 2 eggs putting yolks in pot with the above mixture.

(The yolks can be left out if you want to use up egg whites.)

Place 2 eggs whites in bowl and beat until very firm.

Fold into first mixture.

Place on buttered pan or in buttered casserole.

Sprinkle with paprika or powdered grated cheddar cheese.

Bake at 350 degrees for 10-12 minutes until firm.

DEEP FRIED FISH CAKES (Cod or any white fish)

I learned to make these from a Norwegian lady that lived near us when I was young. She used halibut but any fish is great.

Boil **4 medium potatoes** in salted water until tender.
Drain well and mash.

Add **1 lb. of cod** cut up in small pieces, to the potato.

Add **2 eggs,**

1/4 tsp nutmeg,

1/2 tsp salt,

2 tbsp lemon juice.

Beat with electric mixer until well blended.
A potato masher can be used if you don't have electric power on your boat.

Place **4 cups of vegetable oil** in a 2 qt. pot (It should not be more than half full or it will boil over.)

Heat to 325 degrees on a candy thermometer.

Drop in the fish cake mixture from a soup spoon - about a 2 inch round ball. Cook for 3 to 4 minutes then turn fish balls and cook for 1 or 2 minutes longer, until nicely browned.
Lift out with a spoon and drain on several thicknesses of paper towelling. Keep hot. Makes approximately 18 two inch fish cakes.

These can be fried in a fry pan with a little oil by flattening the fish cakes and then turning them.

CREAMED ONION FISH (Cod or any white fish)**

The following sauce can be poured over any fish and baked.

Dice 2 small onions and set aside.

Melt in the top of a double boiler:
2 tbsp of butter or margarine.

Add 2 tbsp of flour and stir well.

Stir in diced onion and mix well.

Add 1 tsp salt.

Pour in 1 cup of milk and stir continuously until thickened.

Pour the above sauce over approximately 1 lb. of filleted raw fish that has been cut up and placed in the bottom of a buttered bread pan.

Sprinkle with grated cheddar cheese.

Bake at 350 degrees for 30 to 35 minutes for raw fish.
You can use cooked fish but reduce the baking time to 20 to 25 minutes.

The cheese should be nicely browned.

This amount serves 3 or 4.

** You can add pieces of fish to this sauce and cook it on simmer in a double boiler, with the lid on, if you don't have an oven on your boat. If using frozen fish be sure to cook it while it is still partially frozen.

CREAMED PINEAPPLE FISH (Any white fish)

Boil 2 medium potatoes in salted water, drain and mash.

In a bowl mix 1 cup of drained crushed pineapple with

1/2 cup of sour cream,

1 tbsp of white vinegar,

1/2 tsp of salt,

2 tsp of corn starch,

4 tbsp of diced green onion and mix well.

Spread in the bottom of a buttered small casserole.

Place 1/2 lb. of raw fish (approximately 1 cup) cut in pieces over the pineapple mixture.

Put 1-1/2 cups approximately of <u>mashed potato</u> in a bowl and mix with

1 large egg,

2 tbsp of milk,

Dash of seasoning salt,

Dash of salt and mix well. Taste for seasoning.

Spread the potato mixture over the fish and Sprinkle the top with **grated cheddar cheese with skim milk powder.**

Bake at 350 degrees for approximately 35 to 40 minutes.

You can use flaked cooked fish instead of raw fish but just bake for 25 minutes.
This amount serves 4 people.

SCALLOPED FISH (cod or any milk-white fish)**

Place **1 cup of fish** (approximately 1/2 lb. of filleted fish) cut in cubes in a 2 cup measuring cup or bowl.

Dust the cod with **1 tbsp of flour** and then place in the bottom of a buttered bread pan.

Spread **1 can (6-1/2 oz.) of drained tuna**, flaked, on top of the cod.

Place **1 small onion** sliced very thin over the tuna (it won't be cooked if it is sliced too thick).

In a 2 cup measuring cup or bowl put
 1/2 cup of milk

 1/2 cup of mayonnaise,

 1/4 tsp of salt

 1 tbsp of lemon juice and mix well. Pour over fish.

Sprinkle with **grated cheddar cheese with skim milk powder** and Bake at 350 degrees for 30 - 35 minutes until cheese browns slightly.

This amount serves 3 or 4.

Instead of tuna you may use shrimp or crab.

...THANKS A LOT!

** This recipe can be cooked in a double boiler on simmer if you don't have an oven available.

COD LOAF (Or any white fish)**

Melt **1 tbsp** of margarine or butter in the top of a double boiler and remove from heat.

Add **2 slices of soft white bread** cut in small cubes and mix.

Stir in **2 beaten eggs,**

1/4 cup of milk,

1 tbsp of cut up green onion or parsley,

1 tsp of salt,

1 tbsp of lemon juice,

1 tbsp of hot dog relish,

2 cups of cooked flaked cod (approximately 1 lb. of filleted fish).

Place in buttered bread pan and
Sprinkle top with **grated cheddar cheese with skim milk powder.**

Bake at 350 degrees for 20 minutes.

Serve with tartar sauce.

Serves 3 or 4 people.

Raw cod cut in small pieces can be used but allow another 10 minutes cooking time.

* If you are on a boat without an oven this can be cooked in the top of a double boiler on simmer with the lid on the pot.
Cook until firm.

BOUILLABAISSE (Cod or any mild white fish)

1 cup of cod cut into small cubes,

1 cup diced onion (medium onion).

Saute´ the above in **2 tbsp of cooking oil** for two minutes, low to medium heat.

*Add **1 can of mashed stewed tomatoes** (14 oz.).

Simmer until onion is cooked then
Add **1/4 cup of fresh crab meat** (raw or cooked)

1/4 cup of fresh shrimp (raw or cooked)

1 cup of medium dry Sauterne (optional)

Heat and serve immediately. This amount makes a small serving for four.

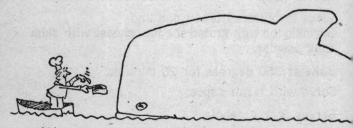

You may vary the type of fish you use in bouillabaisse.

Instead of shrimp and crab you could use limpets, mussels, clams or oysters. Instead of cod you could use any of the mild white fish.

*Stewed Tomatoes contain onion, celery, green peppers, spices -- whereas **canned tomatoes** contain no seasoning.

STUFFED SOLE WITH SEASONED SPINACH (or flounder)

Take **4 sole fillets,** making sure there is no skin left on them as this can be very strong tasting.

Dip fillets in a small bowl in which you have beaten:

1 large egg,

1 tbsp of lemon juice and a

Dash of salt, then....

Dip fillet in another bowl with **1 cup of cracker or bread crumbs** in it.

Put the fillet on a sheet of wax paper and cover it with a layer of **Seasoned Spinach - see recipe.**

Roll fillets up and pin with two or three tooth-picks.

Cover a cookie sheet with foil and butter the foil. Place the rolls on the buttered foil.

Bake at 350 degrees for approximately 30 minutes.

This amount serves four people.

very good

seasoned spinach

on page 31

STUFFED SOLE (or flounder)
WITH CHEESE SAUCE

Take **4 sole fillets** and make sure there is no skin left on them as this can be very strong tasting.
Dip them in a small bowl in which you have mixed:

1/4 cup of vegetable cooking oil,

1 tbsp of lemon juice and

A dash of salt.

Drain for a few seconds and then place them on a dinner plate.

Cover with a layer of **Sole Stuffing - see recipe.**

Roll fillets up and pin with two or three **tooth-picks.**

Cover a cookie sheet with foil and butter the foil. Place the rolls on the buttered foil.

Bake at 350 degrees for 30 minutes.

Remove from the oven and spoon **Cheese Sauce - see recipe,** over each roll and return them to the oven for 5 minutes.

This amount serves 4 people.

Instead of sole rolled, I've used cod cut in thin slices which I place in the bottom of a pan, cover with the stuffing, then another layer of cod. Bake and then cover with cheese sauce.

Melt 4 tbsp of margarine (1/4 cup) in the top of a double boiler.

Cut up into small cubes **4 slices of white bread** and add them to the margarine.

Add **1 tsp of poultry seasoning,**

Dash of salt and

1/2 cup of chopped green onion.

This is enough stuffing for 4 medium fillets.

CHEESE SAUCE FOR STUFFED SOLE

Melt **2 tbsp of margarine or butter** in the top of a double boiler.

Add **2 tbsp of flour** and

1/2 tsp of salt and mix well.

Add **1 cup of milk** and stir continuously until thickened.

Add **1/8 lb. of Imperial sharp cheese** cut in small pieces.

Stir until cheese melts.

Turn heat down to very low, put the lid on the pot and keep the sauce hot until you are ready to spoon it over the Stuffed Sole.

Campbell's Cheddar Cheese soup right from the can may be used instead of the above cheese sauce. It contains cheese, tomato, carrots and seasoning.

Shellfish

CLEANING CLAMS

The clams should be soaked in cold saltwater for 4-8 hours to allow them to spit out the grit and sand in their bodies.

There seems to be a great discrepancy as to the time it takes clams to rid themselves of sand. I checked it out and in 20 to 30 minutes they spit out most of the sand, however, there is still a little bit of grit in them. If you want real clean clams leave them for four hours and change the water at least once and rub the dirt off the shells. Also check to make sure you don't have any duds. They can be left as long as 24 hours if you change the sea water every eight hours and don't have the bucket more than half full of clams but full of sea water.

Don't fill the pail more than half full of clams. They need lots of water to siphon. If crowded they will die. Never eat dead clams.

The larger clams have long siphons or necks and they will squirt water out of the pail all over the floor or counter. Keep them outside where the water will not harm anything. Don't put a lid on the pail as the clams need oxygen.

When the sea water is changed on the clams, rub them clean and try to open each clam by pushing the two sides apart or use your thumb nail. Some pairs of clam shells may be full of sandy mud. (The clam has died or been eaten). Needless to say, if this is cooked with the clams it will open and sand will spoil the pot full.

Another way to clean the clams is to put them in a burlap potato sack or nylon mesh bag and hang them over the side of the boat for a few hours. Tie a rag or string or something to the steering wheel to remind yourself that the clams are there so you don't take off with the clams dragging behind. They will keep for a long time this way providing the water is clean and cold.

If you are staying in a cottage put the clams in a burlap sack and leave them anchored on the rocks - not sand - at about three-quarter tide mark. A bleach bottle filled with sand makes a good anchor. Tie a bleach bottle float to them and then they can be pulled up whenever you are ready to have a feed of clams.

If a clam will not pull in its neck and close when touched, throw it away as it has died.

They will cleanse themselves in fresh water but you lose a lot of nice flavor.

A substitute for sea water when soaking clams is 1/3 cup of salt to 1 gallon of fresh water and for smaller amounts 1-1/2 tbsp of salt to 1 quart of fresh water.

For complete information on how, where and when to catch clams, oysters, mussels, limpets, etc., see our best selling book, *How to Catch Shellfish!*

Horse clams, soft shelled clams and the larger butter clams are cleaned in a manner similar to the razor clam. After the shell is cut away from the flesh, the black portions and green wormlike glands are removed and the body rinsed in running water. The necks should be skinned with a sharp knife while the two tubes of the neck should be cut so they can be flattened for frying.

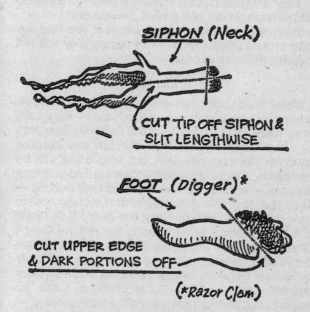

SIPHON (Neck)

CUT TIP OFF SIPHON &
SLIT LENGTHWISE

FOOT (Digger)*

CUT UPPER EDGE
& DARK PORTIONS OFF

(*Razor Clam)

The necks are tougher than the body in many large clams but can be ground up to make good chowder or deep fried fritters. They also make good bait for sole and flounder. (See our popular book, *How to Catch Bottomfish!*)

Cockles and **butter** clams can also be used in chowder or fritters but they are excellent when fried like razor clams.

The **little neck** clam is often called "the steamer" since it is delightful when steam cooked right in the shell. An ideal way to cook them is to put about a 1/4 inch of water in an electric frying pan and steam the clams until they just pop open (usually less than 20 minutes).

They are then dipped in melted butter or ketchup and eaten right out of the shell. Delicious!!!

When you are cleaning the clams if you find any with broken shells throw them out as they will not cleanse themselves of sand.

CAUTION:

Since much has been written about **shellfish poisoning,** prudent caution is a good idea — especially in summer. Dr. D.B. Quayle of the Fisheries Research Board of Canada notes that shellfish can become toxic from sewage pollution, but this danger can be avoided by checking to see that there are no polluting sources — such as sewers or septic tank outfalls — near the shellfish grounds. Unfortunately, waters near populated centers along the entire B.C. Coast can be contaminated — even in the remote Queen Charlotte Islands. Check carefully the *British Columbia Tidal Waters Sport Fishing Guide* issued annually by Federal Fisheries before gathering shellfish from unfamiliar waters. The *Guide* contains some 15 pages listing polluted waters and the list is growing — a dreadful indictment of the way we are treating our environment.

For current local information phone Fisheries and Oceans District Offices. There are eight along the Coast, each with regional offices. Their phone numbers are in the already mentioned *Sport Fishing Guide.*

The other, more serious, **paralytic shellfish poisoning** comes from tiny organisms of the **Gonyaulax** family. In summer, when water temperature, sunlight and nutrients are present in exactly the right combination, these organisms multiply very rapidly. Sometimes the water itself turns reddish-brown, causing what is known as "Red Tide". (Most such Red Tides are not dangerous, being caused by multiplication of harmless plankton.)

All filter-feeding shellfish pump these organisms into their bodies along with their other food. When **Gonyaulax** are present in large numbers, their poison becomes concentrated in the shellfish and can cause serious illness or death if eaten by mammals. (They do not harm the shellfish itself, however!)

Most shellfish lose their toxicity almost completely four to six weeks after a Gonyaulax outbreak. **THE NOTABLE EXCEPTION IS THE BUTTER CLAM, WHICH MAY RETAIN THE TOXIC MATERIAL UP TO TWO YEARS!**

Gonyaulax outbreaks can occur from May to October in the North Pacific — and for even longer periods further south. To protect yourself from possible problems, Dr. Quayle advises as follows (emphasis ours):

"First, it should be ascertained whether there is a ban in effect on the taking of shellfish in the particular area from which they are to be gathered. Local residents are usually aware of this owing to publicity and, in addition, there are the posted warning signs. If there is a ban in effect, **the shellfish specified should not be used under any circumstances.**

"If there is no ban, additional protection may be obtained by proper preparation of the shellfish. Unless it is known that the shellfish to be used are entirely safe, they should be cooked fairly well for heat will destroy some of the poison content. **The nectar or bouillon from the cooking process** should not be used, for any poison in the clam meat, particularly if the siphons are present, will become concentrated in the cooking liquid.

"The **butter clam** is the most abundant and widely used clam in British Columbia. Recalling the fact that most of the toxin in this species is contained in the **siphon** and **gills**, these should be removed before cooking. Thus the butter clam should be opened fresh like an oyster.

"This then leaves five pieces of meat, the body, two adductor muscles and two mantle muscles (see illustration). These meats may then be cooked in the usual manner, although chowder preparation causes more reduction of toxicity in butter clams than does frying. Raw clam parts, obtained as

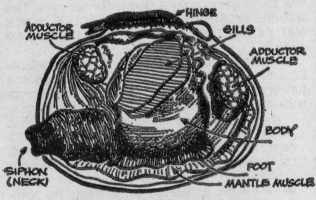

1. OPEN CLAM BY SLIDING KNIFE BETWEEN SHELLS AND SEVERING EACH ADDUCTOR MUSCLE.

2. REMOVE BODY, ETC., FROM SHELLS. CUT OR PULL MANTLE MUSCLES OFF. BODY AT EACH END NEAR ADDUCTOR MUSCLES.

3. REMOVE ADDUCTOR MUSCLES.

4. STRIP OFF AND DISCARD THE SIPHON AND GILLS.

5. REMOVE AND DISCARD THE DARK DIGESTIVE GLAND FROM THE TOP OF THE BODY.

EDIBLE PARTS OF BUTTER CLAM

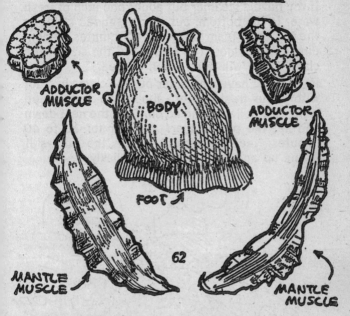

ADDUCTOR MUSCLE

BODY

ADDUCTOR MUSCLE

FOOT ↑

MANTLE MUSCLE

MANTLE MUSCLE

62

described, when compared to similar parts from whole steamed clams are less toxic, so raw shucking of butter clams is recommended.

"It must also be remembered that the amount of toxin, when present, is proportional to the amount of shellfish meat, so the dose of poison is proportional to the amount of meat eaten.

"If these precautions are carefully observed, the risk of being poisoned by clams is very much reduced."

STEAMED CLAMS

If you have a steamer put about one inch of fresh water in the bottom, put the de-sanded clams in the top and steam for 30 to 40 minutes, depending on the amount of clams and the size of the clams. They will open when cooked.

If you don't have a steamer put the clams in a pot with some fresh water, about two inches and bring to a boil with the lid on. Turn the heat down and set the pot lid ajar. Simmer for 30 to 40 minutes. Keep a watchful eye on the pot as it foams up and boils over very quickly.

While the **clams** are cooking **melt some butter** to dip them in as you take them out of the shell. A little **drop of lemon** added to the butter or a little **Seasoning Salt** added to margarine is nice.

I like to use a double boiler for melting the butter as it stays hot while people are eating the clams.

Give each of the clam eaters a little pyrex custard cup or a small aluminum tart cup to put the butter in. Dip each clam in this as it is removed from the shell. I serve bread and butter or hot rolls with the clams.

The broth from steaming or boiling the clams is delicious served in a mug. Use the small clams for eating right out of the pot and save the large clams and broth for making clam chowder.

PRESSURE COOKING CLAMS

Place the pressure cooker rack in the bottom of the pan and pour in one cup of water. Fill the pressure cooker two-thirds full of clams. Bring the pressure up to the top ring or band (15 lbs. pressure). "Presto", (my brand of cooker,) refers to it as the "Cook Position". Reduce the heat enough to keep the pressure at this level for ten minutes for small clams and fifteen minutes for larger clams. The broth will be strong so add water for your chowder, according to your own taste. Keep your eye on the pressure cooker heat or you will have clams all over the ceiling.

BASIC CLAM CHOWDER (for four)

1 cup of cut up clams

Cut the neck off the large clams as they are very tough.

2 cups of clam broth, (This is salty!)

1 medium potato diced into little cubes,

1 medium onion diced.

Get the above ready then start to fry, in the pot in which you are going to make the chowder,
2 slices of side bacon cut into small pieces.

Fry the bacon until crisp, stirring constantly. Now drain off the excess fat. If you burn the bacon, throw it out, wash the pot and start over. Add chopped onion and saute for about two minutes. Add broth, potato and cut up clams. Simmer until the potato and onion are cooked.
Take your choice of **Tomato Flavoured Chowder, Creamed Tomato Chowder** or **Creamed Chowder Without Tomato** - see recipes.

TOMATO FLAVORED CHOWDER

Basic Clam Chowder (for four),

Add **1 can of tomato soup** (10 oz.) and

1 can of water

CREAMED TOMATO CHOWDER

Basic Clam Chowder (for four)
Add **1 can of tomato soup (10 oz.)**
1 can of cream (6 oz.)
4 oz. of water
or
10 oz. of fresh cream
(A NO - NO! Once you add the cream do not boil
the chowder or the cream will curdle. It doesn't
hurt the flavor but it ruins the looks!)
Use the top of a double boiler to heat the chowder
so you don't boil it or burn it.

CREAM CHOWDER WITHOUT TOMATO

Basic Clam Chowder (for four)

Add **1 can of cream (16 oz.) or fresh cream**
Use a double boiler or make-shift double boiler -
see index.

TO FREEZE BASIC CLAM CHOWDER

Triple the recipe for Basic Clam Chowder if you
want to freeze some of it. Leave the basic clam
chowder on the stove until an inch of the water
steams away. Fill one-pound plastic containers
with this mixture to within one inch of the top,
cover and freeze immediately. Label and date.
(Stays good up to two months) To use the frozen
basic clam chowder let it thaw for half an hour
then empty it into a pot. Add an equal amount of
water (or less — depending on how rich you like
it) and then any of the variable mixtures (see
recipes).

CLAM STEW

Use a double boiler or make-shift double boiler -

Melt **2 tbsp of margarine or butter,**

Add **2 tbsp of flour,**

1/2 tsp of salt and stir together

Pour in **1 cup of cream** (or milk if you are watching calories)

Stir continuously until thickened then add **1/2 cup of small clams** or cut up larger clams. Remember to cut off the tough neck.

About three minutes before serving add **1/4 cup of cut up green onions.**

CHOMP!

These are nice served as a hot appetizer or they can be made larger for a main entree.

1/2 cup of cut up clams which have been steamed, simmered or pressure cooked.

Drain then fold into.

2 eggs whipped with a fork

Add a **pinch of salt** (not too much as there is salt in the clams)

Spoon a teaspoonful on to a low heated frypan with a small amount of butter or margarine melted on it. Fry until firm then turn and cook for another minute. Serve hot and as soon as possible. Drain on paper towelling.
These are nice served with small crackers.

LOBSTER

When you buy a live lobster from the fish market tank be sure it is lively and active — never eat a dead lobster. The large claws are pinned shut with wood pegs so you will not get bitten. Look to be sure the pins are there.

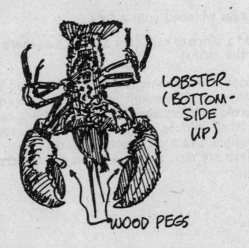

LOBSTER (BOTTOM-SIDE UP)

WOOD PEGS

After you purchase or catch a lobster take it home immediately and put a large pot of water on to boil. Add approximately 1 tablespoon of salt to the water. Bring to a full rolling boil then plunge the live lobster head first into the pot. It can be given a crack between the eyes with a hammer if you are squeamish about cooking it alive. When the **water comes back to a boil** set the minute minder for 7 minutes for a 1½ pound lobster and up to 10 minutes for a 2 pound one. Do not over-cook or the meat will become rubbery.

When cooked, pour the boiling water off the lobster and let it cool for a few minutes. When cool enough to handle pull the two large claws off and discard any of the sponge like, hairy, pale beige, triangular shaped lungs that pull out with the claws. Now take hold of the tail and pull it off of the body and set it aside with the claws.

Cut the under side of the body open down the middle to within an inch of the head. Do not cut the sack below the head. Keep the grey-green and coral parts as they are edible. Remove and dispose of the sack from below the head. Pick and wash away the grey-brown spine out of the body.

Pull the legs off each side of the body, then remove and dispose of the sponge like, hairy, pale beige, triangular shaped lungs. Pick off the lobster meat from the joints. It is almost impossible to get the meat out of the pencil like legs but you can bite and suck the juice out. The white egg-like substance is edible.

Crack the claws and remove the meat. Slit the membrane down each side of the under side of the tail and remove the tail meat. The tail meat can be put back in the shell for serving to add a decorative touch.

PARTS OF A LOBSTER

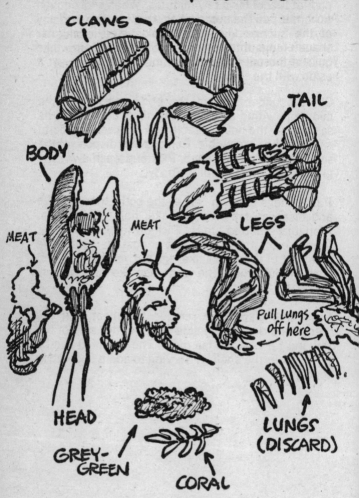

CLAWS

TAIL

BODY

MEAT

MEAT

LEGS

Pull Lungs off here

HEAD

GREY-GREEN

CORAL

LUNGS (DISCARD)

SAM'S BROILED LOBSTER TAILS

Allow the raw **lobster tail** to thaw in the fridge, overnight, then run a sharp knife down either side of the underside of the shell. Pull away the membrane you have loosened and pull the meat from the shell.

Cut the lobster meat partially lengthwise. Season with **salt** and **butter**. Broil **covered with foil**, for approximately 10 minutes. Uncover the lobster and broil for an additional 5 minutes.

Serve with **melted butter** seasoned with **garlic powder** or **seasoned salt** or **Worchestershire sauce** or **lemon pepper.**

CREAMED LOBSTER

Make the following sauce in a double boiler.

Melt **2 tbsp of margarine or butter** in the top.

Add **2 tbsp of flour.**

½ tsp salt and mix together.

Pour in **1 cup of milk or cream** and stir until thick.

Add **2 tbsp of diced green onion** and

1 diced hard boiled egg.

Stir in **1 diced lobster tail** and cook for 5 to 10 minutes in the double boiler. Serve on **toast or rice.**

LOBSTER NEWBERG

Boil ½ cup of long grain white rice in salted water for 15 minutes and drain. (It is not so apt to boil over if you add 1 tsp of cooking oil to the water).

Add 2 tbsp of chopped green pepper to the drained rice and mix well. (If you don't care for green pepper use green onion).

Keep the rice hot in a casserole while you make the Lobster Newberg.

Melt 2 tbsp of margarine or butter in the top of a double boiler.

Add 1/8 tsp Seafood seasoning,

¼ tsp salt,

1 raw diced lobster tail

Cook the tail with the cover on, at medium heat, 5 to 10 minutes.

If you won't be ready for the Newberg right away turn the heat under the double broiler to simmer.

Beat 2 egg yolks in a bowl and add

½ cup of cream, canned or fresh.

Have 2 tbsp of medium dry sherry on hand.

5 minutes before you are ready to serve, stir the sherry into the lobster then add the egg yolk and cream mixture and stir continuously until thickened.

Pour over the hot rice and serve immediately.

This amount serves 2 or 3 people.

Remove the Lobster Newberg from the heat the minute it thickens or it will separate. This won't hurt the flavor but it spoils the looks.

The egg whites keep well covered in the fridge and can be used to dip fish or chops in when you are coating them with crumbs. They can be added to scrambled eggs or use them in an egg nog.

LOBSTER AND RICE CASSEROLE

Boil ½ cup of long grain rice in salted water for 15 minutes.

Drain and place in the bottom of a small buttered casserole. Keep hot.

Prepare ½ **cup of diced celery** and

1 tbsp of chopped green pepper or parsley.

In the top of a double boiler melt

2 tbsp of margarine or butter.

Add **2 tbsp of flour** and

½ tsp of salt and mix well.

Add **1 cup of milk** and stir continuously until thickened.

Turn heat under double boiler to simmer.

Add **1 tbsp of ketchup,**

1 tbsp of cheese spread or grated cheese.

Add prepared **celery** and **green pepper**

Stir in **1 raw diced lobster tail.**

Pour over the rice and sprinkle the top lightly with **paprika.**

Bake at 350 degrees for approximately 20 minutes.

This amount serves 3 or 4 people.

Boil ½ **cup of long grain rice** in **salted water** for 15 minutes.

Drain and place in a serving dish, keep hot.

Make the following curried sauce in a double boiler.

Melt **2 tbsp of margarine or butter** in the top.

Add **2 tbsp of flour**

½ **tsp salt**

½ **tsp of curry powder** and stir together (this is very mild).

Pour in **1 cup of milk or cream**

Add **2 tbsp of ketchup**

Stir continuously until thickened then add

1 raw diced lobster tail and cook over double boiler for 5 to 10 minutes.

Serve over **hot rice or over a toasted bun.**

This amount serves 3 or 4 people.

MUSSELS

BLUE MUSSELS

These can be pulled off the rocks and steamed open or opened by slipping a paring knife down the crack between the shells.

There is a crunchy fibre, with which they attach themselves to the rocks, that is hard to see and take off. If you miss it on the small mussels don't fuss as it can be eaten.

Serve the steamed mussels with a little melted butter. The raw mussels can be used in bouillabaisse, or they can be sauteed in a little butter and served with small crackers.

BEST TIME TO EAT OYSTERS

The best time for picking and eating oysters is from mid-November until mid-May. In cold water, the oysters can remain firm and tasty well into June.

Seasonal changes in taste are most notable if the oysters are eaten raw. If they are cooked, and especially if they are barbecued in the shell, these taste changes are less obvious.

If you are not opening the oysters right away keep them in a pail of sea water in a cool and shady place. They can be kept in a potato sack or mesh bag hanging in the water over the side of the boat. Remember not to take off on a jaunt dragging them behind.

Move starfish away from any oysters or clams you have on the beach or rocks. They love them and eat them by covering the oyster and sucking on the shell until the oyster gets tired and opens.

Oyster drills and augers also love oysters and clams, so move them away from your supply. If you find a clam or oyster shell with a perfectly round hole in it you know a drill or auger has had a good meal.

SHUCKING OYSTERS

This is the most difficult part of the whole oyster gathering process for most people. However, shucking oysters is really a very simple task if you learn something about the physical characteristics of an oyster.

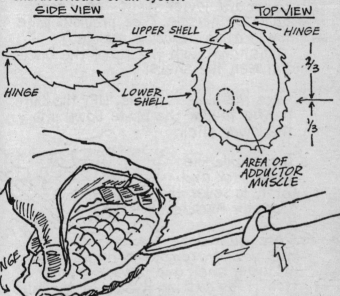

SIDE VIEW

UPPER SHELL

HINGE

LOWER SHELL

TOP VIEW

HINGE

2/3

1/3

AREA OF ADDUCTOR MUSCLE

HINGE

1. WEAR A HEAVY GLOVE! BE CAREFUL! THE KNIFE IS *SHARP* AND MIGHT SLIP!
2. Put oyster, rounded side (lower shell) down, on a steady working-surface. Hold in place with fingers of left hand around the edge as shown above.

RIGHT-HANDED SHUCKERS KEEP THE HINGE-END TOWARD YOU...

83

Continued next page....

...LEFT-HANDED SHUCKERS SEE
DIAGRAM AT BOTTOM OF PAGE.

3. Insert the tip of the knife between upper and lower shells-- near the adductor muscle. (See previous page for locating adductor muscle.) Twist and push the tip of the blade between the shells.

4. Once the blade is inside, LIFT the knife handle to aim the blade DOWN into the lower shell.

5. Then move the knife back and forth to sever the adductor muscle.

6. Once you've done this, you can remove or open the upper shell and free the meat from it by cutting the adductor muscle where it attaches to the shell.

'SOUTHPAW' SHUCKERS....

HINGE →

Place shell, round side down, with the hinge end AWAY from you.
Then follow steps 3 thru 6 above.

84

OYSTERS IN STEWED TOMATOES

Melt **2 tbsp of butter or margarine** in the top of a double boiler.

Add **2 tbsp of flour** and

1/4 tsp of salt and mix well.

Pour in **1 can (14 oz.) of Stewed Tomatoes** (these are seasoned and have onion, celery and green pepper in them)

Stir continuously until thick.

Place **1/2 lb. (8 medium) drained oysters** in the bottom of a buttered bread pan.
Pour the tomato sauce over the oysters.

Sprinkle with **grated cheddar cheese.**

Bake at 350 degrees for 20 to 25 minutes.

This amount serves 3 or 4.

You can add the oysters to this sauce and cook them on simmer in a double boiler, with the lid on, if you don't have an oven on your boat. If the oysters are frozen be sure to cook them while they are still partially frozen.

OYSTERS ROCKEFELLER

Place drained oysters in a buttered casserole or pan.
Cover with Seasoned Spinach - see recipe.
Bake at 375 degrees for 15-20 minutes.
These can be cooked in the deep side of an oyster shell if you want to be fancy.

STEAMED OYSTERS

Wash the oyster shells off and place in the top of the steamer. Pour one inch of water in the bottom of the steamer. Steam **oysters** anywhere from 30 to 45 minutes depending on the size and amount. They will open when cooked.
Serve with **Relish Sauce, Cheese Sauce** or **Butter Sauce** for baked or barbecued oysters — see recipe.

BARBECUED OYSTERS

If you have the barbecue going and want a few **oysters** as appetizers place them on the rack, deep side of the shell on the bottom and they will open about 1/16" when cooked. There is the odd one that will not cooperate so you have to pry it open with the oyster knife. Garnish with one of the **sauces** listed for Baked Oysters. Some people like them well cooked and some like them just hot.

RAW OYSTER COCKTAIL

Open **oysters,** wash and drain on paper towelling. Cut larger oysters in small pieces and garnish with a spoonful of the **Relish Sauce.** Serve with **crackers.** People who love raw oysters will eat them out of the shell without anything on them.

BAKED OYSTERS

People love these because they don't have to open them. Wash any sand or dirt off the un-shucked **oysters** before you place them in a roasting pan. Place the deeper half of the shell on the bottom. This will hold the moisture so the oyster will steam open. Place them in a 450 degrees oven and cook until the shell opens. It takes anywhere from 15 to 20 minutes depending on the size of the oyster. There is the odd oyster that will not cooperate and pop open so you have to give it a little pry with your oyster knife. Remove the pan of oysters from the oven and take the top shell off leaving the oyster in the larger bottom half.

The following are goodies I put on them and then place the oysters back in the oven for five minutes.

Relish Sauce or **Cheese Sauce** or **Butter Sauce** - see recipes.

BUTTER SAUCE FOR BAKED OR BARBECUED OYSTERS

Melt **2 tbsp of butter** and add a scant **1/4 tsp of lemon juice.**

Spoon over the oysters. If you like you can add a dash of **garlic powder** or **onion salt** to the butter. Pop them back in the oven to get hot for about 5 minutes - 450 degrees.

RELISH SAUCE FOR BAKED OR BARBECUED OYSTERS

Mix half **tomato ketchup** and half **barbecue hamburger relish** in a cup. Spoon a little bit on top of each oyster before putting them back in the oven for five minutes - 450 degrees.

CHEESE SAUCE FOR BAKED OR BARBECUED OYSTERS

Melt **2 tbsp of margarine or butter** in the top of a double boiler.

Add **1-1/2 tbsp of flour,**

1/2 cup of grated strong Canadian cheddar cheese
(or 1/8 lb. of Imperial Sharp cheddar),

1/2 tsp of salt,

1 cup of milk and stir continuously until thickened.

Spoon a little bit on top of each oyster before putting them back in the oven for five minutes - 450 degrees.

This sauce can be kept in a jar in the refrigerator.

Campbell's Cheddar Cheese soup right from the can may be used instead of the above cheese sauce. It contains cheese, tomato, carrots and seasoning.

FRIED OYSTERS

As you shuck the oysters put them into a bowl. Fill the bowl with cold water and gently wash the loose broken bits of shell off the oyster. Drain on several thicknesses of paper towelling. Keep in a covered bowl in the refrigerator until you are ready to cook them.

Whip **1 egg** in a small bowl with a fork.

Add a very small dash of **salt**.

In another bowl put **1/2 cup of dried bread or cracker crumbs**.

Dip the oysters in the egg and then the crumbs and fry at a low to medium heat until golden brown. Sprinkle a dash of **salt** on as they fry in a small amount of **vegetable oil**. Turn to brown on all sides. They can also be deep fried. Drain on paper towelling and keep hot.

Serve with **Mock Tartar sauce** or **ketchup.**

FRIED OYSTERS WITH BACON

Take a strip of **side bacon** and wrap it around the shucked oyster meat and fasten it with a tooth pick through the **oyster**. If the strips of bacon are long, a half strip is usually enough to go around the oyster. No salt is needed here as there is plenty in the bacon. Fry at a low to medium heat turning until the bacon is cooked on all sides. Drain on paper towelling. Serve with tartar sauce or ketchup.

If you have lots of time and don't mind fussing you can dip the oysters in **beaten egg and bread** or **cracker crumb** mixture—then wrap them in the bacon strip. These look and taste terrific.

OYSTER STEW

Use a double boiler or make-shift double boiler. Melt **2 tbsp margarine or butter,** in the top,

Add **2 tbsp of flour,**

1/2 tsp of salt and stir together.

Pour in **1 cup of cream** (milk if you are watching your calories).

Stir continuously until thickened and then add **6** or as many as you wish, **small oysters.**

You can cut up larger oysters but when you put them in the stew don't stir them around until after they have cooked enough to set. The stew will turn grey if you stir the cut up oysters too soon.

Cook for approximately five minutes.
About three minutes before you serve the stew

Add **1/4 cup of cut up green onions.**

FREEZING OYSTERS

Shuck fresh live oysters and place oysters and liquor in a bowl. Wash oysters free of broken shell in their own liquor. Do not drain. Pack in plastic containers that are liquid tight. Strain liquid and cover oysters with same. You may have to add a little **water** to cover them completely. Leave 1/2 inch for expansion. Label and date. Seal and freeze immediately. Store at 0 degrees F.

Cut the meaty parts away from the shell and clean everything off the muscle. Wash in cold water, dry on paper towelling. I use a carpenter's wooden mallet to pound the abalone until tender. You have to break the fibres down, so really whack it on a wooden cutting board. It can be sliced first by cutting across the grain into 1/2" slices and then pounded until limp. It can be sauteed in butter after pounding, or it can be dipped in beaten egg and then in bread or cracker crumbs and fried in vegetable oil at a low to medium heat. Sprinkle a dash of salt on each side as you fry it.

Well known fisherman-author Charlie White tells me he cooks abalone without pounding and finds it very tender. It is sliced thin against the grain and then sauteed in a little butter with a sprinkle of salt.

ABALONE STEW

Pour into a pot:
1 can of condensed tomato soup (10 oz.) and 1 can of water,

Add **1 medium potato** cubed into small pieces,

1 medium onion diced,

1 tsp of butter and

1 cup of abalone, pounded and cut into cubes.

Simmer until potato and onion are cooked.
Serve with crackers.

ABALONE PATTIES

These are nice served as a hot appetizer or they can be made larger for a main entree.

1/2 cup of cut up pounded abalone folded into **2 eggs** that have been whipped with a fork.

Add a **pinch of salt.**

Spoon a teaspoonful on to a frypan over low heat, with a small amount of butter or margarine melted on it. Fry until firm then turn and cook for another minute. Drain on paper towelling. Serve hot and as soon as possible. These are nice served with small crackers.

There are two kinds of scallops in B.C. waters. The purple hinged rock scallop and the sand scallop. The purple hinged one attaches itself to rocks and remains stationary. The sand scallop can propel itself from the sand through the water to avoid enemies.

WOOOSH!

WAS IT SOMETHING I SAID...?

Use an oyster knife to open the scallop shell. Cut the muscle away from the shells. This is the part you eat. Clean the muscle off and discard the rest of the scallop. The colour of the muscle can vary from white to a light orange. Cut the scallop into thin slices across the grain. Saute in butter or dip in beaten egg and bread or cracker crumbs and fry at a low to medium heat in vegetable oil or butter until golden brown. Scallops are nice with Hollandaise Sauce over them.

SCALLOP PATTIES

1/2 cup of sliced scallops (against the grain)

2 eggs that have been whipped with a fork.

Add a **pinch of salt**.

Spoon a teaspoonful on to a low heated frypan with a small amount of butter or margarine melted on it. Fry until firm then turn and cook for another minute. Serve hot and as soon as possible. Drain on paper towelling.

These are nice served as an appetizer with small crackers.

Make them bigger for an entree.

SCALLOPS WITH CHEESE SAUCE

Saute Scallops in butter and add 2 tbsp of medium dry Sauterne

And a dash of salt.

Place in the bottom of a buttered casserole or in individual shells.

In the top of a double boiler
Melt 2 tbsp of margarine or butter.

Add 1-1/2 tbsp of flour and mix.

Pour in 1 cup of milk and stir until thickened.

Add 1/8 lb. Imperial sharp cheddar cheese and blend.

Pour the cheese sauce over the scallops and Bake at 350 degrees for 10 minutes or until lightly browned.

SHRIMP

These delicious morsels can be bought uncooked by the pound if you happen to know
when the shrimp boats come in to dock. Better
still, catch them yourself. See Heritage House
book, *How to Catch Shellfish*.

Take your own plastic bag, pot or pail. If you use
a plastic pail be sure it hasn't been used to hold
gas, oil or resin as the smell stays in the plastic
no matter how many times it is washed and then
the taste is transferred to the shellfish. Take the
shrimp straight home and put a pot of sea water
on your Coleman stove, outside, and bring to
a boil.

You can use salted fresh water (1/4 cup salt to 1
quart of water) but the flavor of the cooked
shrimp isn't as good. You can cook seafood in
the house but be prepared to air the place well
when you finish.

Put the small shrimp in the boiling water and
cook for two minutes from the time the water
returns to the boil. Drain and let cool. Do not
rinse with cold water as this washes a lot of the
flavor away.

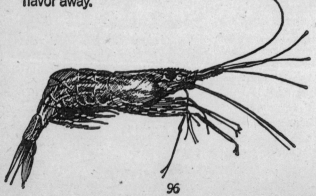

To clean, break off and keep the tail section of the shrimp. Discard the rest.

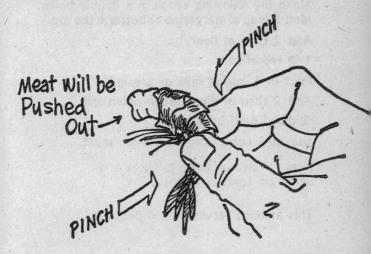

Meat will be
Pushed
Out →

PINCH

PINCH

Pinch the tail section between your fingers as illustrated here, and the shrimp meat will literally pop out! Use this for the following shrimp recipes!

Buy raw shrimp for deep frying in Deep Fried Puffy Batter (recipe page 152). The raw shrimp is cheaper.
A friend from New Orleans told me that we clean the shrimp at the wrong time. The meat is tough and the shell soft when raw and it reverses when they are cooked so clean them when raw.
Charlie White cleans his shrimp and prawns before cooking by simply digging his thumb into the body just at the joint between body and tail. Then pull the tail and it breaks away cleanly. Cook the tails only (with their shell covering) which fit in a much smaller pot.

CREAMED SHRIMP

Make the following sauce in a double boiler.
Melt **2 tbsp of margarine or butter** in the top.

Add **2 tbsp of flour,**

1/2 tsp of salt,

Pour in **1 cup of milk or cream,**

Add **2 tbsp of diced green onion** and

1 diced hard boiled egg,

Stir in **1 cup of cooked shrimp meat.**

Heat for two or three minutes and
Serve on **toast** or on **rice.**

This amount serves 3 or 4 people.

SHRIMP SALAD

Cut or tear the **lettuce** into pieces.

Add a little cut up **green onion, diced celery,**

Canned **green peas** or fresh frozen peas boiled in
salted water for one minute only.

Add shelled **shrimp** and toss with mayonnaise.
Pile this on lettuce leaves on a platter.

Garnish with **tomato wedges, asparagus spears,
cucumber** slices and **sweet pickles** or **pickled
sliced beets.**

I serve this salad with hot **Cheese Biscuits** — see
recipe.

CURRIED SHRIMP

Make the following curried sauce in a double boiler.

Melt **2 tbsp. of margarine or butter** in the top,

Add **2 tbsp of flour,**

1/2 tsp of salt,

1/2 tsp of curry powder and stir together (this is very mild).

Pour in **1 cup of milk or cream,**

Add **2 tbsp of ketchup.**

Stir continuously until thickened then add **1 cup of shrimp** and heat for two or three minutes.

Serve with hot **rice** or over a **toasted bun.**

This amount serves three or four people.

SHRIMP COCKTAIL

(Chill shrimp!)

Place shelled shrimp in a small glass or dish and add a small amount of the following:

Mayonnaise mixed with a little **ketchup** or

Salad dressing mixed with a little **ketchup** or **Mock Tartar Sauce** — see recipe.

A NO - NO! Don't drown the lovely subtle flavor of the shrimp by using a hot tomato sauce.

SHRIMP NEWBERG

Boil **1/2 cup of long grain white rice** in salted water for 15 minutes. (It is not so apt to boil over if you add:
1 tbsp of cooking oil to the water.)

Add **2 tbsp of chopped green pepper** to the drained rice and mix well.

Keep the rice hot in a casserole while you make the Shrimp Newberg.

Melt **2 tbsp of margarine or butter** in the top of a double boiler.

Add **1/8 tsp of Seafood seasoning,**

1/4 tsp of salt,

1 cup of shelled shrimp (Approximately 4 oz)

Heat with cover on at medium heat

If you won't be ready for the Newberg right away turn the heat under the boiler to simmer.

Beat **2 egg yolks** in a bowl and add

1/2 cup of cream, canned or fresh.

Have **2 tbsp of medium dry sherry** on hand.
5 minutes before you are ready to serve,
Stir the sherry into the shrimp then

Add the egg yolk and cream mixture and
Stir continuously until thickened.

Remove immediately from the heat the minute it thickens or it will separate. This won't hurt the flavour but it spoils the looks.

This amount serves three or four people.
(The egg whites can be used to dip fish in when you are coating it.)

SHRIMP AND RICE CASSEROLE * *

Boil **1/2 cup of long grain rice** in salted water for 15 minutes.

Drain and place in the bottom of a small buttered casserole or buttered bread pan.

Get ready **1/2 cup of diced celery** and
1 tbsp of chopped green pepper or parsley.

In the top of a double boiler melt
2 tbsp of margarine or butter

Add **2 tbsp of flour** and
1/2 tsp of salt, and mix well.

Add **1 cup of milk** and stir continuously until thickened.

Turn heat under double boiler to simmer.

Add **1 tbsp of ketchup,**
1 tbsp of cheese spread
celery and green pepper.

Stir in **1 cup of shelled shrimp.**

Pour over the rice and sprinkle the top lightly with **paprika.**

Bake at 350 degrees for approximately 20 minutes.

This amount serves 3 or 4 people.

* * This food can be eaten without baking if you are on a boat and don't have an oven. I finish it off in the oven because it makes it look more appetizing.

Salmon

Salmon and Grilse recipes may be used for Steelhead and Trout.

HOW TO CLEAN SALMON

1. Insert knife tip into anal vent and slice the thin layer of skin along the belly... to a point under the eyes.

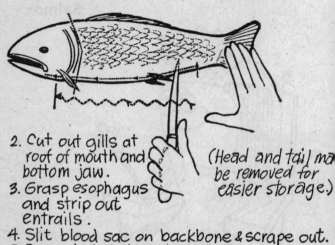

2. Cut out gills at roof of mouth and bottom jaw.

(Head and tail may be removed for easier storage.)

3. Grasp esophagus and strip out entrails.
4. Slit blood sac on backbone & scrape out.
5. Rinse lightly in cold water.

HOW TO FILLET SALMON

(cutaway showing knife angles & placement)↘

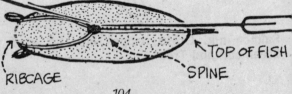

RIBCAGE   SPINE   ←TOP OF FISH

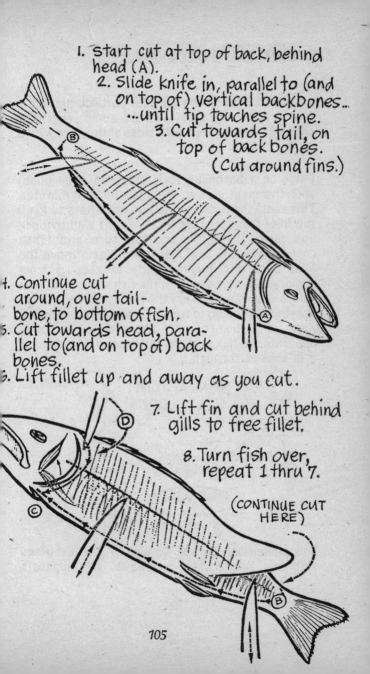

1. Start cut at top of back, behind head (A).

2. Slide knife in, parallel to (and on top of) vertical backbones... ...until tip touches spine.

3. Cut towards tail, on top of back bones. (Cut around fins.)

4. Continue cut around, over tail-bone, to bottom of fish.

5. Cut towards head, parallel to (and on top of) back bones.

6. Lift fillet up and away as you cut.

7. Lift fin and cut behind gills to free fillet.

8. Turn fish over, repeat 1 thru 7.

(CONTINUE CUT HERE)

BARBECUED SALMON FILLETS

Leave the skin on the fillet for barbecuing. Add a few drops of lemon juice to some vegetable cooking oil and brush both sides of the fillet with a pastry brush.

Place on a barbecue rack (that has been oiled) with the meat side to the coals for two minutes. This seals the juice in. Use two egg lifters to keep the fillet from sticking by moving it slightly back and forth. Oil skin side. Now turn and finish cooking with the skin side down. Again move the fillet back and forth slightly to keep it from sticking. Do not over cook the fish while the meat side is down as it will dry the fish out and it will fall apart when you go to turn it. The salmon is cooked when the transparent appearance is gone. Separate the flakes at the thickest part to check if it is cooked through.

Fellow Saltaire author Charlie White disagrees with my barbecuing technique. He suggests cooking the salmon **skin side down** until the fat begins to "milk" (ooze out from the top as a milky white thick liquid). Then he turns the fillet and finishes it off by browning the meat side for one or two minutes only. He claims this produces a moist, fully cooked meat which is never over cooked.

If you are doing a fish over fifteen pounds use a couple of inexpensive flat cookie sheets to turn the large fillet. Put one cookie sheet under the large fillet and the other on top, turn and slide the fillet back onto the barbecue. Baste with lemon and oil and keep moving fillet for a few minutes to stop the skin from sticking to the rack.

One can improvise by using chicken wire, which incidentally does not get hot and is, therefore, easily removable. Make an envelope of chicken wire with fish (steak, fillet or whole) in the center. It is then very easy to turn. Be sure to oil it first.

Do not use frozen fish for barbecuing as the outside layer becomes tough and dried out before the inside is cooked. For whole fish look inside around the spine to see if it is cooked all the way through

NOTE Before eating Salmon....
We suggest removing the band of dark meat that runs along the center of either side of the fish, next to the skin. Many people find it can give the fish an "off" taste, otherwise.

SMOKING ON THE BARBECUE

15 - 20 minutes before cooking put a handful of hickory chips (buy at any hardware store) in water to soak. Make 'boats' of foil for salmon steaks or fillets. Make sure foil does not touch

LID OR COVER OF FOIL

GREEN ALDER BRANCHES, CUT UP, MAY BE USED FOR SMOKING. (REMOVE LEAVES.)

FILLETS

FOIL "BOATS"

HICKORY CHIPS

BARBECUE

sides of fish to ensure maximum surface for smoking. Season fish with salt and spread a thin covering of brown sugar over the top surface. Leave for 15 minutes to become syrupy. The coals should be covered with a grey ash. Put soaked hickory chips on the coals. Place the foil 'boats' on the rack and cover barbecue. If your barbecue does not have a lid improvise one with a sheet of foil and cover so there is a good amount of space between the salmon and the foil for smoke to circulate and so that no smoke escapes. Leave, without peeping, for 10 - 15 minutes, depending on the thickness of the fish. This is a scrumptious way of barbecuing fish and so easy.

TO FREEZE SALMON FILLETS OR STEAKS

Wash fillets or steaks in cold water.
Drain and blot dry with paper towelling.

WRAP
< FILLET
WRAP
< FILLET
WRAP

Separate fillets or steaks with plastic wrap —
(waxed paper gets wet and mushy) or
Wrap the whole amount in plastic wrap and then
in foil or freezer wrap.
Label and date and then freeze immediately.
Be sure and cook frozen fillets and steaks before
they are completely thawed.
Use within two months to prevent its becoming
stale.

SALMON STEAKS

A large salmon is needed for these. Cut the steaks
the thickness desired. Dip in flour and fry in a
vegetable cooking oil.
Sprinkle with a little salt on both sides as it cooks.
Use a medium hot pan. Do not overcook as salmon
becomes very dry.
Serve with tartar sauce and slices of fresh lemon
or lemon juice.
Cut filleted salmon into pieces and fry the same
way the steaks are done.
The salmon can also be dipped in beaten egg and
then in bread or cracker crumbs.

SALMON GRILSE OR TROUT UNDER ONE POUND

Clean the fish, then:
Dip in flour and fry in vegetable cooking oil.

Sprinkle a little salt on both sides as it fries.

Look inside to see if it is cooked.
It will look raw around the spine if it is not cooked.

To remove the bones after cooking cut along the center back of the fish. Take hold of the spine with your fingers and gently lift while taking a tableknife to push the fish away from the bones. Turn and do the same on the other side. The bones will come away leaving the fish boneless if this is done carefully. Each individual can bone his own fish or they can be done before the meal and returned to the frypan or an oven to keep hot. Serve with **Mock Tartar Sauce** (see recipe page 32), fresh **lemon slices** or **lemon juice.**

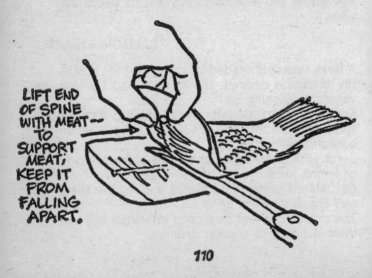

LIFT END
OF SPINE
WITH MEAT—
TO
SUPPORT
MEAT;
KEEP IT
FROM
FALLING
APART.

SALMON TOMATO RICE CASSEROLE * *

Boil **1/2 cup of long grain white rice** in salted water for 15 minutes. Drain and set to one side.

Get ready **1/4 cup of sliced celery,**

1/4 cup of diced green onion and

1 cup of flaked cooked salmon (approx. 1/2 lb.).

In a pot pour **1 can (14 oz.)** of tomatoes and heat at medium to high temperature. If the tomatoes are whole cut them in pieces.

Add **1/2 cup of mayonnaise** and mix well.

Add **1/2 tsp of salt** and
1/4 tsp of seasoning salt,

celery, green onion, salmon and rice.
Mix well and simmer for 2 minutes.

Pour the salmon and rice mixture into a buttered casserole or buttered bread pan.
Sprinkle the top with **Cheese Cracker Topping -** see recipe.

Bake at 350 degrees for approximately 12 to 15 minutes.
This amount serves 3 or 4 people.

The above food can be eaten without baking if you are on a boat and do not have an oven. The reason I finish it off in the oven is that it looks more appetizing and it can be served piping hot.

DEEP FRIED SALMON CAKES

I learned to make these from a Norwegian lady that lived near us when I was young. She used halibut but any fish is great.

Boil **4 medium potatoes** in salted water until tender.
Drain well and mash.

Add **1 lb. of salmon** cut up in small pieces, to the potato.

Add **2 eggs,**

1/4 tsp of nutmeg,

1/2 tsp of salt,

2 tbsp of lemon juice.

Beat with electric beater until well blended.
(A potato masher can be used if you don't have electric power on your boat.)

Place **4 cups of vegetable oil** in a 2 qt. pot (it should not be more than half full or it will boil over).

Heat to 325 degrees on a candy thermometer.

Drop in the fish cake mixture from a soup spoon - about a 2 inch round ball. Cook for 3 to 4 minutes then turn fish balls and cook for 1 or 2 minutes longer until nicely browned.

Lift out with a perforated spoon and drain on several thicknesses of paper towelling. Keep hot.
Makes approximately 18 two inch fish cakes.
These can be fried in a pan with a little oil by flattening the fish cakes and then turning them to brown on both sides.

SALMON IN CELERY CHEESE SAUCE * *

Boil **1/2 cup of long grain rice** in salted water for 15 minutes.
Drain and place in the bottom of a buttered bread pan or small casserole.

In the top of a double boiler heat
1 can(10 oz.) of cream of celery soup and

1/4 cup of milk and mix well.

Add **1/2 cup of frozen green peas,**

1 tbsp of chopped green onions,

1/4 cup of cheese whiz,

1 cup of flaked cooked salmon (approx. 1/2 lb.)

Simmer for 2 minutes.

Pour this mixture over the rice and
Sprinkle the top with **Cheese Cracker Topping -
see recipe.**

Bake at 350 degrees for 12 to 15 minutes.
This amount serves 3 or 4 people.

** This recipe can be cooked in a double boiler on simmer if you don't have an oven available.

SALMON TURNOVER FILLING

Chop finely **1 cup of cooked salmon** and

1 hard boiled egg together in a bowl.

Watch for and pick out small bones.

In the top of a double boiler on the counter
Stir **1 tsp of corn starch** into
1/2 cup of milk and mix.

Now put the pot over the heat.
Stir continuously until thickened.
(If you are interrupted before it is thick, take it off
the heat and set it in a cool place).
Turn the heat to simmer under the double boiler.
Beat in prepared salmon and egg.

Add **1 tbsp of margarine or butter** and

2 tbsp of mayonnaise,

1 tbsp of pickle relish or chopped sweet pickle.

Add a **dash of salt** to taste and set aside to cool.
This is enough filling for 16 - 4" circle turnovers.

While the above is cooling make the **Salmon
Turnover Pastry - see recipe.**

TURN
OVER,
SALMON!

SALMON TURNOVER PASTRY

In a bowl place **2-1/4 cups of pre-sifted flour.**
(Use it right out of the bag, do not re-sift).

Add **1 tsp of salt.**

1/2 tsp of poultry seasoning,

2 tbsp of grated cheddar cheese with skim milk powder.

Put **3/4 cup of hard margarine** in the bowl with the flour and cut it into small pieces.
Take off your rings, clean your nails, scrub your hands and then crumble the mixture with your finger tips.

Cut in **1/2 cup of cold water** and then blend with your fingers.
Roll out the pastry to an 1/8" thickness and cut out circles with a large can or saucer.

Wet the edges of each circle of pastry with cold water so they will seal together when cooked.

Put a spoonfull of **Salmon turnover filling - see recipe, on half of the circle of pastry. Fold the pastry over the filling and seal the edges.**

Cover a cookie sheet with foil. Do not butter it.
Place the turnovers on the foil.

Prick the top of each turnover twice with a fork to let the steam out. (If you forget to do this and you did a good job of sealing the edges the turnovers could pop).

Bake in a 375 degrees oven for 15 to 20 minutes until a light golden colour.
Use the left-over pastry as a crust for a fish or chicken casserole or it can be frozen by putting it in and sealing a plastic sandwich bag).

SALMON CHOWDER

Put the bottom of the double boiler on to simmer as you will need it in a few minutes to keep the chowder hot.

Dice **1 medium onion** (approximately 1 cup) and Dice **1 medium potato** (approximately 1 cup).

Cut fish into small pieces (approximately 1 cup).

Cut into small pieces **2 slices of side bacon**
Fry bacon in top half of double boiler at medium heat.

Pour off excess fat.

Add fish and saute for 1 minute.
Add onion and saute for 1 minute.

Add **1 cup of water**

Add potato and let simmer until vegetables are cooked.

Place pot in top of double boiler and
Add **2 cups of milk or cream**

Add 1/4 to 1/2 tsp of salt to taste.

Serve when hot. Do not boil.

The above amount makes a generous serving for six.

Cut the **buns** in half and butter them.

Mix **1** cup of flaked cooked **salmon** with

1 diced hard boiled **egg,**

1 tbsp of pickle relish or chopped sweet pickle,

2 tbsp of **mayonnaise** and a

dash of salt. Mix well.

Spread filling on a bun halves and place buns on a cookie sheet.

Bake at 350 degrees for 10 minutes.

This mixture also makes a nice filling for plain or grilled sandwiches.

FLUFFY SALMON OMELET

Get a cookie sheet ready by covering it with a sheet of foil and then butter the foil. (This saves a lot of washing and scrubbing.

Turn the oven on to 350 degrees.

Have the frying pan ready at low to medium heat (250 degrees on an electric frying pan).

Melt **1 tbsp of margarine or butter** in the frying pan.

Separate **3 large eggs** putting the yolks in one bowl and the whites in the second bowl.

Into the yolks add:
3 tbsp of milk and beat well.

Add a generous **1/4 tsp of salt,**

1 tbsp of corn starch,

1 tbsp of finely chopped green pepper,

1 tbsp of finely chopped green onion,

1/2 cup of flaked salmon and mix well.

Beat the egg whites until very firm with clean beaters.

Pour the yolk mixture on top of the whites and lightly fold until blended.

Pour the omelet into the frying pan and cook over a low heat until the omelet is set. (250 degrees on an electric frying pan for 3 to 5 minutes).

Cut the omelet in four and place it on the buttered foil with an egg lifter.

Bake at 350 degrees until lightly brown on top, about 6 minutes.

Serve immediately. This is enough for two people. This is very tasty served with tartar sauce.

If you use small eggs cut back on the salt to a scant 1/4 tsp.

SALMON ROE [CAVIAR]

The next time you find roe in a salmon you have caught prepare it in the following manner. Wash it off in cold water then pour boiling water over it to blanch the roe. Pick the membrane off the eggs and then chill the eggs in the fridge. Spoon onto crackers and drizzle with fresh lemon juice or soya sauce. This recipe comes from Japan where salmon eggs are considered a real delicacy.

STUFFED BAKED SALMON, STEELHEAD OR TROUT

Stuffing for a five pound salmon:

Melt in a fry pan 1/4 lb. of margarine or butter.

Dice 2 small or 1 large onion and saute.

Add 1 tbsp of sage or poultry seasoning and mix.

Pour the above over one half loaf of white bread which has been cut in small cubes. Mix well.

I like to fillet the salmon before I put the stuffing in as it makes it easier to serve and the stuffing can be placed along the full length of the fish.

Place a large piece of foil in the bottom of the roasting pan.

Place one fillet on this, skin side down. Spread the stuffing on top and place the second fillet on this with skin side up.

Fold the foil up and over the fillets to hold everything in place. I leave the ends open a little bit to let some of the steam out otherwise the stuffing gets too soggy. Bake at 325 degrees for one hour approximately.

When stuffing a whole salmon place the stuffing in the stomach pouch and hold it in place with the foil you wrap it in. Leave the ends open a little bit to let the steam out.

Using this method you don't have to sew up the salmon.

If you find Steelhead or Trout a little dry, cook a strip or two of side bacon with it. This adds a nice flavor as well as moisture.

SALMON SCALLOPED FISH * *

Place **1 cup of salmon** (approximately 1/2 lb. of filleted fish) cut in cubes in a 2 cup measuring cup or bowl.

Dust the salmon with **1 tbsp of flour** and then place in the bottom of a buttered bread pan or small casserole.

Add **1 can (6-1/2 oz.) of drained tuna**, flaked, on top of the salmon.

Top with **1 small onion** sliced very thin (it won't be cooked if it is sliced too thick).

In a 2 cup measuring cup or bowl put
1/2 cup of milk,

1/2 cup mayonnaise,

1/4 tsp of salt,

1 tbsp lemon juice and mix well.

Pour over fish.

Sprinkle with **powdered grated cheddar cheese** and

Bake at 350 degrees for 30 to 35 minutes until cheese browns slightly.

This amount serves 3 or 4 people.

Instead of tuna you may use shrimp or crab.

If using frozen fish or shellfish be sure to cook it while it is still partially frozen.

** This recipe can be cooked in a double boiler on simmer if you don't have an oven available.

SALMON LOAF **

Melt **1 tbsp of butter or margarine** in the top of a double boiler
and remove from heat.

Add **2 slices of soft white bread** cut in small cubes and mix.

Stir in **2 beaten eggs**

1/4 cup of milk

1 tbsp of cut up green onion or parsley.

1 tsp salt

1 tbsp lemon juice

2 cups of cooked flaked salmon (approximately 1 lb. of filleted fish).

Place in buttered bread pan and
Sprinkle top with **grated cheddar cheese.**
Bake at 350 degrees for 20 minutes.

Serve with **tartar sauce.**

Serves 3 or 4.

Raw salmon cut in small pieces can be used but allow another 10 minutes cooking time.

** If you are on a boat without an oven this can be cooked in the top of a double boiler on simmer with the lid on the pot. Cook until firm. If using frozen fish be sure to cook it while it is still partially frozen.

Cut up **1 lb. of salmon** into pieces and place in the bottom of a buttered casserole.

In a bowl put **1 can of celery soup**

1/4 cup of milk

1/4 cup of cheese whiz

1 tbsp chopped green onions

Mix the above ingredients well and pour over fish in casserole.

Sprinkle top with **paprika.**

Bake at 350 degrees for 30-35 minutes approximately.

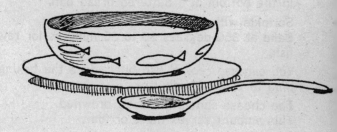

** This can be cooked in a double boiler on simmer if you are on a boat and don't have an oven.

CREAMED ONION FISH (Salmon) *

The following sauce can be poured over any fish and baked.

Dice **2 small onions** and set aside.

Melt in the top of a double boiler **2 tbsp of butter or margarine.**

Add **2 tbsp of flour** and stir well.

Stir in diced onion and mix well.

Add **1 tsp salt.**

Pour in **1 cup of milk** and stir continuously until thickened.

Pour the above sauce over approximately **1 lb. of filleted raw fish** that has been cut up and placed in the bottom of a buttered bread pan.

Sprinkle with **grated cheddar cheese.**
Bake at 350 degrees 30 to 35 minutes for raw fish.

You can use cooked fish but reduce the baking time to 20 to 25 minutes.

The cheese should be nicely browned.
This amount serves three or four.

If using frozen fish be sure to cook it while it is still partially frozen.

* You can add pieces of fish to this sauce and cook it on simmer in a double boiler, with the lid on, if you don't have an oven on your boat.

FISH SOUFFLE (Salmon)

In the top of a double boiler melt
2 tbsp of butter

Add **2 tbsp of flour**

Dash of nutmeg or curry

1/2 tsp of salt

Stir in **3/4 cup of milk** and stir constantly until thick.

Remove from stove and stir in
1/4 cup dried bread or cracker crumbs and
1 cup of cooked flaked fish

Separate **2 eggs** putting yolks in pot with the above mixture. (The yolks can be left out if you want to use up egg whites.)

Place 2 eggs whites in bowl and beat until very firm.

Fold into first mixture.

Place on buttered pan or in buttered casserole. Sprinkle with **paprika or powdered grated cheddar cheese.**

Bake at 350 degrees for 10 - 12 minutes until firm.

BOUILLABAISE (Salmon)

1 cup of salmon cut into small cubes.

1 cup of diced onion (Medium onion)

Saute the above in **2 tbsp of cooking oil** for two minutes, low to medium heat.

Add **1 can of mashed stewed tomatoes**(14 oz.)*

Simmer until onion is cooked then
Add **1/4 cup of fresh crab meat,**

1/4 cup of fresh shrimp,

1 cup of medium dry Sauterne (optional).
Heat and serve immediately. This amount makes a small serving for four.

You may vary the type of fish you use in bouillabaisse. Instead of shrimp and crab you could use limpets, mussels, clams or oysters.

You can also improvise a bouillabaisse by using various leftovers from a big dinner or barbecue.

*Stewed Tomatoes contain onion, celery, green peppers, spices -- whereas **canned tomatoes** contain no seasoning.

HOW TO MAKE A SALMON SMOKER

You will need an old refrigerator, one to two feet
of stove pipe, an electric hot plate, a large cast
iron frying pan and a small barrel or tin box large
enough to house the hot plate, frypan and alder.

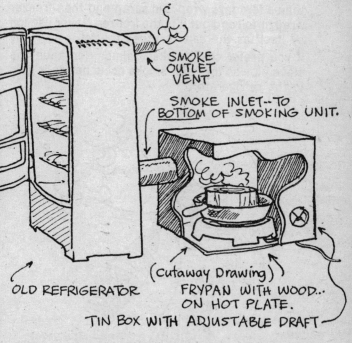

SMOKE OUTLET VENT

SMOKE INLET--TO BOTTOM OF SMOKING UNIT.

OLD REFRIGERATOR

(Cutaway Drawing)
FRYPAN WITH WOOD..
ON HOT PLATE.

TIN BOX WITH ADJUSTABLE DRAFT

Connect the tin box or barrel to the refrigerator
box by using stove pipe one to two feet in length.
Leave sufficient opening at the bottom of the tin
box for draft. Place a four inch thick round slab of
alder wood in the frying pan. Turn on the hot

plate. Check periodically to make sure the alder is not flaming and to see if you need to put more alder on the frying pan. Smoking should take approximately six hours depending on how dry you like the smoked salmon.

When cool take it off the foil. Take the skin off and package the smoked salmon. Better still, eat some! Wrap it in saran wrap first and then in foil or freezer wrap. To keep smoked salmon for more than a few days wrap it in saran and then freezer wrap or foil and put it in the freezer. Never use foil by itself as the salt corrodes the foil.

If you prefer cold smoked salmon, lengthen the stove pipe so the that smoke cools before it gets to the refrigerator.

HOW TO SMOKE SALMON

To make the brine mix equal parts of **rock or pickling salt** and **brown sugar**. Add water and mix to a watery paste. For example 1 cup of salt, 1 cup of brown sugar and 1/2 cup of water.
Mix enough to cover fillets.

Clean and scale the salmon. Cut off the head, tail and fins. Fillet the salmon but leave the skin on. Cut up the fish into six pieces if it is less than five pounds and if the salmon is from five to ten pounds cut it into eight pieces.

Try to make the pieces about the same size so they all will be done at the same time. Put the pieces of salmon in the brine to soak over-night. After soaking over-night lightly rinse the brine off in fresh cold water. Drain on paper towelling, blot dry and smoke by placing the pieces of salmon, skin side down on pieces of aluminum foil that have been cut slightly larger than each piece of fish. This prevents them from sticking to the smoke house rack. Leave small spaces between each piece of salmon so the smoke can get at all edges.

Exotic Recipes For Adventurous Chefs!

LIMPETS

OYSTER DRILLS

BARNACLES

DULSE

SEA URCHIN

These can be gathered at low tide from off the rocks or you can find them under live oysters.

Let them clean themselves in fresh sea water for 30 minutes. Put them in boiling sea water or salted fresh water (1-1/2 tbsp salt to 1 qt of tap water) for two minutes from the time the water **returns** to the boil. Hook them out of the shell with a darning needle and pull the operculum off — the **drills** hatch door.

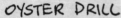

OYSTER DRILL

Dip in **melted butter** to which you have added a little **sage** or **poultry seasoning**. Serve with **melba toast**. Dip to toast in the melted seasoned butter. These taste a little like escargot.

BARNACLES

BARNACLES

Look for the one-to-two-inch barnacles quite low on the beach, usually in a protected crack of rock. Pry them off with a sharp knife. I hit the end of my paring knife with a rock to get them off. You have to cut the meat off the rock also. Clean the seaweed and loose shell off the barnacles then place them upside down in a pan of rock salt. Dot with slivers of butter and bake at 350 degrees for 10 minutes for 1 to 2 inch barnacles. My son, Jim, has brought them up when skin diving and they have been 4 to 5 inches high and in large clusters. These taste a lot like an oyster but have the consistency of scrambled egg. They are delicious. I tried one raw and if you like raw oysters you will like raw barnacles.

You can find sea cucumbers at a 1-ft. tide or less in around rocks and weed in bays or lagoons. The small ones are under the rocks. A fairly large sea cucumber is needed if you are going to cook its muscle. Cut the ends off and pour the insides out. Now cut the cucumber down one side and open it out. Pull and cut the white muscle away from the skin. Wash the muscle in cold water, drain on paper towelling and blot dry. Pound well with a wood mallet on a cutting board then cut into very small pieces. Saute in butter and serve on crackers or use in Sea Cucumber Patties. This has a mild flavour much like scallop but is tougher so really pound it.

Sea cucumbers will, when attacked, disgorge their internal organs (to confuse the enemy, who is left eating the insides) while the cucumber escapes to grow new ones. This will usually happen when you pick one up, so don't be alarmed -- it's the cucumber itself (outside part) you want, to cook the muscle.

SEA CUCUMBER PATTIES

1/2 cup of finely chopped and pounded sea cucumber muscle.

Add to **2 eggs** that have been beaten with a fork.

Add a **pinch of salt.**

Spoon a teaspoonful on to a low heated frypan with a small amount of butter or margarine melted on it. Fry until firm then turn and cook for another minute. Serve hot and as soon as possible. Drain on paper towelling.
Serve as an appetizer with small crackers.

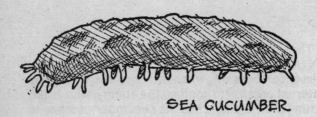

SEA CUCUMBER

You find these in water below low tide in holes in the rock. A skin diver can bring them up for you. Take the sea urchin and break open the bottom centre, but cutting around it with a sharp knife. Pull the round bone–like Aristotle's lantern out. Wash with cold water or sea water and shake all the loose insides out. There is a light brown roe clinging to the sides of the shell. This is what you eat.

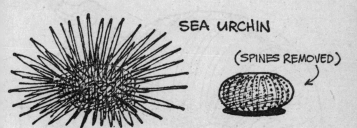

SEA URCHIN

(SPINES REMOVED)

The sea urchin roe can be eaten raw on crackers or it can be sauteed in a little butter and served on crackers. This is a real delicacy like caviar. There isn't very much roe in a four inch sea urchin, just enough for a taste.

If you want to keep the shell this roe can be poked and shaken out. The shell is very fragile so be careful. To keep the shell simmer it in hot water for five minutes and then gently brush the spines off and finish washing the insides out. Set the shell in a bowl of fine sand, gently, and bury it leaving only the opening in the bottom showing. Make a soupy mixture of plaster of paris and water and pour it in this opening until the shell is full. Gently tamp it in with a small stick. This will dry overnight. The sea urchin shell makes a nice paper weight or souvenir.)

MOON SNAIL

My son was skin diving and brought up a sea urchin so he could take pictures of it for me. He also brought up a moon snail so decided after examining the large muscular foot that I would try that on them for dinner. Break the shell with a rock and remove the broken shell from the snail.

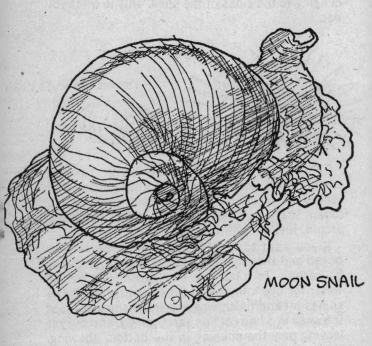

MOON SNAIL

Cut the muscular foot off and cut the operculum (its door) away. Slice it very thin across the grain and pound it to paper thinness. Saute it in a little butter. As it cooked it shrank back to its original thickness. I found it tasty, mild like scallop but not the nice texture of scallop. It was tough and chewy. We all agreed that it was a shame to destroy the nice shell.

If you want a lovely souvenir, place the moon snail in a pot of boiling water and let it simmer for ten minutes. You can then pull the cooked snail out by very gently pulling on the operculum. If you don't get it all out — it curls down to a fine point — put it down on the beach or in the rocks in a protected spot and the little crabs will clean it out overnight for you. Small children love to put the shell to their ear to hear the roar of the ocean.

I used to put my oyster drill shells down in the rocks to be cleaned out by the little crabs but discovered one day when I was snorkelling that I was supplying the hermit crabs with nice new homes. Saw one of my nice orange oyster drill shells scurrying across the bottom with Mr. Hermit Crab in it. Up to this time I had been blaming the kids for taking them.

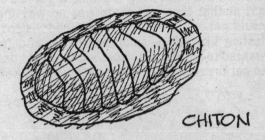

CHITON

Last summer a skin diver brought a giant chiton up for me to try. Cut the muscle out and clean it off. Slice it very thin across the grain and pound it until paper thin. Saute in a little butter. It has a flavor not unlike scallop but like the moon snail it is tough and chewy. The smaller chitons are a little better but you really have to pound them. They are found at low tide under rocks and under empty shells. You have to pry them off with a knife.

DULSE (Fucus)

This is the reddish brown seaweed that is so common on the seashore. It has the yellow pods that pop when you step on them. My father told me they ate dulse over in Scotland. I was a young girl at that time and there was no way that he could get me to eat any of it. I had visions of it tasting like iodine smelled. Charlie and Nelson wanted to know more about seaweed so I decided to get brave and try some of the dulse seaweed.

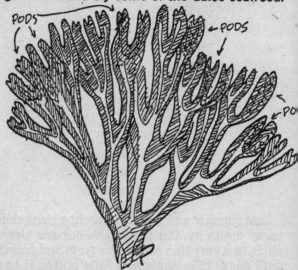

What a surprise! Raw right off the beach the dulse was delicious — not at all strong tasting. It is very bland and chewy and a little bit salty. I kept breaking off another piece and chewing on it.

The top two or three inches are the most tender and I picked the part that hadn't started to puff up. The puffs were full of a gelatine like substance which is probably algin that they use in thickening cake mixes and puddings, etc.

Blanch the seaweed by pouring boiling water over it in a strainer. It turns a beautiful dark green. Pack the dulse in small jars and pour the same vinegar mixture over it that is used for Japanese Seaweed (see recipe page 144).

You can use this as a pickle or mix it in with your regular lettuce salad.

Dry the dulse on a cookie sheet covered with aluminum foil after blanching it with boiling water in a strainer. Dry it in a warming oven and put it in a sealed jar to keep. It is lovely and crisp and very tasty as a nibbler. It could also be dried on a heat tray or out in the summer sun.

Save the **vinegar** off any sweet cucumber pickle, blanch the dulse, pack it in a clean jar and cover it with the vinegar. It keeps well in the fridge.

SEA LETTUCE (Ulva Lactuca)

After trying dulse and being pleasantly surprised I decided to try the sea lettuce. Again it was delicious. It tasted very bland like salty lettuce. It could be mixed in with your salad, fresh off the beach. Sea lettuce is a beautiful green colour and grows at about half tide mark.

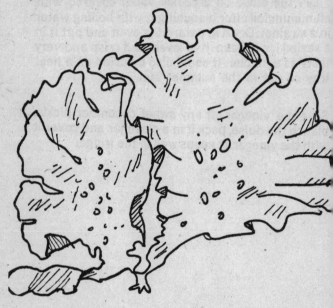

I tried pickling the sea lettuce but it went soft and mushy.

My Japanese friends in Hawaii use the sea lettuce to wrap their rice cakes. This is boiled rice rolled up in the sea lettuce and served with soya sauce. The sea lettuce was very small at Easter when I tried it so you would have to mix it with the cooked rice. In the summer time the leaves are much larger.

For drying sea lettuce blanch it by pouring boiling water over it in a strainer. Spread it out on a sheet of aluminum foil on a cookie sheet and put it in a warming oven or on a heat tray to dry. It could also be put out in the sun during the summer. It is lovely and crunchy but breaks up into small pieces when you try to get it off the foil. It could be used to season salads or as a nibbler like potato chips.

PICKLED JAPANESE SEAWEED (Sargassum)

Pick the Japanese seaweed when it is young, around Easter Time. It goes to seed in the summer months.

Wash the seaweed in fresh water and pick it over. Put **4 cups of seaweed** in a strainer,

Pour **4 cups of boiling water** over it and then leave to drain.

Simmer in a pot for two minutes with the following,

   1 cup of cider vinegar,

   1 cup of brown sugar and

   1/2 tsp of salt.

Remove this from the heat and cool, then add
1/4 cup of fresh finely slivered cucumber

1/4 cup of finely grated raw carrot,

.4 cups of blanched seaweed,

2 tbsp of Saki (optional)

Mix well and keep it in a glass jar. It will keep for
two days this way but if you want to keep it longer
don't add the cucumber and carrot until the day
you want to serve it.

I've tried freezing the seaweed but it discolours
and goes soft and mucky. Since then I've been told
by a Japanese friend that it can be dried and that
it will keep this way for a long time. Soak it in
water and it is ready to use in the above recipe.

GLASSWORT
(Also known as "Crowfoot Greens" or "Chicken Claws".)

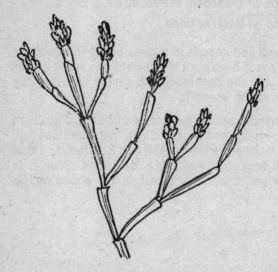

Look for these in sheltered inlets, lagoons or bays. They grow just above the high-water mark. Pick the choice green part but leave some to go to seed.

Wash in cold water and pick out any grass.

Cook in a small amount of salted water for 2 minutes.

Drain and season with a small amount of butter.

These are finger eating greens as they have a tough inner stem that you discard. They are a little bit like asparagus in flavour.

LIMPETS

Leave them in fresh sea water for 30 minutes so they can rid themselves of any grit, especially if you take them off of sandstone rocks.

These may be sauteed in a little butter and served with crackers.

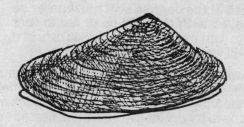

LIMPET PATTIES

These are nice as a hot appetizer.

1/2 cup of cleaned limpets (Pound large ones to tenderize).

2 eggs that have been whipped with a fork.

Add a **pinch of salt.**

Spoon a teaspoonful on to a low heated frypan with a small amount of butter or margarine melted on it. Fry until firm then turn and cook for another minute. Serve hot and as soon as possible. Drain on paper towelling.

These are nice served with small crackers.

DOGFISH OR PACIFIC SHARK

I remember reading in the paper that North American fisheries were exporting dogfish to the market in Europe and I had heard that dogfish are used for fish and chips in England. After asking around, this is the information I came up with:

There is urea in the skin, blood and flesh of the dogfish so it must never be cooked with the skin on or fed to your pets with the skin on. It can kill cats and it will make humans very sick.

We were jigging for cod and caught two dandy dogfish. I had to do a lot of talking but finally convinced my husband that he should let me keep one to try cooking it. I cleaned, filleted and skinned it right in the boat and then washed the fillets off over the side and slipped them into a baggie. It is a nice white fish but the texture is not as flaky as cod.

I cooked it by dipping it in **beaten egg,** then in **dried bread crumbs,** sprinkled it lightly with **salt** and then fried it in a little **cooking oil.** I had

ARF!

to admit it tasted very much like cod and that people wouldn't know the difference if they weren't told. We have been so indoctrinated into thinking that dogfish is an ugh! fish that the only way we'll get people to eat it is to come up with another name. How about SUBMARINE FISH or GODFISH (dog backwards)?

The dogfish eats nothing but the best fish in the ocean! I've had them take a chunk out of a salmon I was reeling in and another time one tried to swipe a codfish I had on my line.

To cook dogfish use any of the recipes in this book for Bottomfish — they'll never know the difference.

Remember! Clean, fillet and skin your dogfish immediately! (See pages 34-5 for filleting). Do not leave it sitting around and do not put it in the fish box with other fish. The acid in the skin could contaminate them. Beware of the sharp spines in front of each center back fin.

NOTE: Although we have never noticed any ammonia flavour in dogfish prepared the way already described (filleting and washing in salt water immediately it is caught) there will be a problem if fish are left uncleaned. The reason is that the urea causes the release of ammonia as the fish ages or cooks. The antidote is to simply soak the fillets overnight in a weak solution of vinegar or lemon juice. If neither is available, salt water will substitute, as will one cup of salt in one gallon of fresh water.

CAUTION: Canada's Federal Fisheries Department recommends that only dogfish under 24 inches (60 cm) be eaten. The reason is that larger — hence older — fish have been around long enough to build up relatively high levels of mercury. (Just another example of how we are ruining our environment.)

DEEP FRIED DOGFISH CAKES

Boil **4 medium potatoes** in salted water until tender.

Drain well and mash.

Add **1 lb. of dogfish** cut up in small pieces to the potato. (Remove all bones from fish.)

Add **2 eggs,**

1/4 tsp nutmeg,

1/2 tsp salt,

2 tbsp lemon juice.

Beat with an electric mixer until well blended. Use a potato masher if you don't have elec. power aboard.

Place **4 cups of vegetable oil** in a two-quart pot (no more than half full or it will boil over).

Use a **candy thermometer** to measure the heat of the oil. Try to keep it no lower than 325 degrees and no higher than 375 degrees.

Slip in the fish cake mixture from a soup spoon — about a two-inch round ball. Cook for three to four minutes then roll fish cakes and cook for one or two minutes longer, until nicely golden.

Lift out with a slotted spoon and drain on several thicknesses of paper towelling. Keep hot. Makes approx. 18 two-inch cakes.

These can be fried in a fry pan with a little oil by flattening the fish cakes.

SCALLOPED DOGFISH * *

Place **1 cup of dogfish** (approx. 1/2 lb. of filleted fish) cut in cubes in the bottom of a buttered bread pan. Dust with **1 tbsp of flour.**

Spread **1 can [6 1/2 oz.] of drained tuna,** flaked, on top of the dogfish.

Slice **1 small cooking onion** very thin (it won't cook

if too thick) and place over the tuna.
(Substitute 2 tbsp of dried onion or 4 tbsp of fresh green onion chopped for the cooking onion.)
In a bowl mix **1/2 cup of milk**
1/2 cup of mayonnaise
1/4 tsp of salt
1 tbsp of lemon juice
Pour over fish and sprinkle with **Kraft grated cheddar cheese** and bake at 350 degrees for 30-35 min. until cheese browns slightly.
This amount serves 3 or 4.
Instead of tuna you may use **shrimp or crab**.
**(This recipe can be cooked in a double boiler on simmer if you don't have an oven available.)

DOGFISH WITH MUSHROOM SOUP * *

Cut up **1 lb. of dogfish** (approx. 2 cups) into pieces and place in the bottom of a buttered casserole.
In a bowl mix
1 can Campbell's Cream of Mushroom soup — 10 oz.
1/4 cup of milk,
1/4 cup of soft cheese spread [Cheez Whiz]
1 tbsp of chopped green onion.
Pour over the fish in the casserole and sprinkle the top with **Kraft grated cheddar cheese**.
Bake at 350 degrees for 30-35 min. approx.
For a change crumble **2 slices of crisply cooked bacon** and add instead of the cheese spread.
(I fry up a pound of side bacon at a time, real crisp, drain it well on paper towelling, crumble it into little pieces and store it in a small baggie in my freezer. This is very handy to have on hand as a garnish — just take out what you need.)
**(This recipe can be cooked in a double boiler on simmer if you are on a boat and don't have an oven.)

DEEP FRIED PUFFY BATTER

This recipe comes from Denny Boyd, author of the humorous cook book "Man On The Range".

1 cup pre-sifted flour
1 tsp baking powder
1 tsp salt
2 tbsp vegetable oil
1 cup cold water
2 egg whites (Use yolks for an egg nog)

For batter, mix flour, baking powder, salt, oil and water, stirring just until combined. Let stand 20 minutes in order to give the baking powder time to act. Otherwise it breaks down the egg white and you lose the "puffy".

Beat egg whites until firm and fold gently into flour mix. Coat article you are deep frying in flour before you dip it in the batter.

This recipe can be used for deep frying cauliflower, broccoli, onion rings, chicken, shrimp, etc. It is a terrific recipe as it is so light and puffy. Pour **4 cups of vegetable oil** in a 2-quart pot (no more than half full or it will boil over). Try to keep the temperature of the oil (candy thermometer) no lower than 325 degrees and no higher than 375 degrees.

Strain oil into jars when cold, seal and keep in fridge.

HERRING

Clean **herring** but save the **roe** as this is delicious sauteed in a little **butter**.

This is a very bony fish but if you take the bones out as illustrated on page 110 there won't be many left.

FRIED HERRING — Dip in **flour** and fry in a little **vegetable cooking oil** with a **dash of salt** on both sides.

SMOKED HERRING (KIPPERS) — Split herring in two and open out.

For smoking see HOW TO SMOKE SALMON page 127-9.

SPLIT HERRING BY CUTTING DOWN BACK, ALONG AND PARALLEL TO SPINE & BACKBONE...

LEAVE "HINGE" OF SKIN AT STOMACH..

... OPEN OUT

COOKING KIPPERED HERRING — Pour **boiling water** over **kipper,** let stand for 5 minutes then drain. Cook in a 450 degree oven for 3 or 4 minutes to heat thru. Serve for breakfast with **toast** or for dinner with a **baked potato.**

PICKLED RAW HERRING — This recipe comes from my Danish friend Sven. Clean and fillet **8 large herring.**
Simmer to dissolve **7 oz white sugar** in **10 oz wine vinegar** and **10 oz water.**

When cool add **2 Bay leaves, 6 peppercorns, 2 med. onions** sliced thin, **2 tbsp of dill, 2 tbsp parsley** and **1 tsp tarragon leaves.**
Cut herring in bite sizes and pack in jars alternating onion slices and herring and cover with liquid. Keep in a cool place for 2 days before using. Keeps for 10 days. Serve herring and onion slices with **thin slices of bread.** Herring and onion slices may be served in **sour cream.**

OCTOPUS

Rub the tentacles with salt before cooking to get rid of the slime. Rinse off excess salt but leave a little on for seasoning.

Octopus can be steamed or simmered until tender. The time depends on the size of the tentacle. Larger tentacles require longer cooking time. The larger tentacles can be sliced against the grain and pounded to tenderize them. The skin can be removed from the larger tentacles after it has been cooked. Drain well as there is a lot of gelatin in octopus. When cool, cut into thin slices across the grain or at a slight angle. It will be tough otherwise.

Octopus can be served with the Hollandaise Sauce (recipe page 26) hot — or cold with Hollandaise Mousse (recipe page 28), — or with Mock Tartar Sauce (recipe page 32).

DEEP FRIED OCTOPUS

Cut **octopus** in small pieces, dip in **flour** and then in **Deep Fried Puffy Batter** . Follow cooking instructions for deep frying. (recipe page *152* .)

SKATE

This is a salt water fish of the ray family with a broad flat body. The "wings" have a central frame of gristle covered with meat.

Sprinkle with salt and steam for 6 to 8 minutes or simmer for 4 to 6 minutes depending on size.

Let cool in the fridge then pick the flesh from the gristle and bottom skin. There is a fair amount of waste. (The top skin had been removed when I bought the skate at the fish market.)

Skate has a mild flavor like white fish so it can be used in any of the recipes for Bottomfish. The Hollandaise Sauce (recipe page 26) was delicious over it. My family and guests thought they were eating crab as it does have a slight crab like flavor.

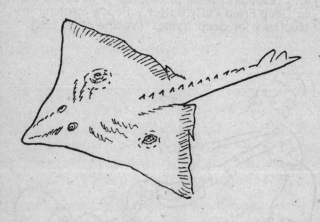

SMELT

These are very small needle-like fish that spawn in the sand on the beaches in and around rivers in the early spring. At this time they can be gathered very easily. Clean and cook as follows. The **roe** can be eaten raw on a **cracker** with **lemon juice** or **soya sauce** drizzled over it or sauteed in a little **butter.**

HOW TO DE-BONE SMELT

Maria from the Seven Seas Fish Market showed me how to do this. She learned to do it back in Greece.

Cut the head and tail off the smelt then clean the fish. Cut the fish tail open down to the spine. Now run your thumb, inside, pressing hard, along the spine the full length of the smelt and then along the ribs on both sides.

Take hold of the spine at the head end and it and the ribs pull away from the fish without a bone being left. Give each fin a pull — they come off easily. The one at the center back is a little harder to get out but you can feel when you have all the bone out.

Wash **de-boned smelt** under cold water and blot dry with paper towelling.

These are delicious dipped in **oil** with a little **lemon juice** in it and then dipped in **flour** and fried in **vegetable oil** seasoned with a little **butter** and a sprinkle of **salt.**

They can be stuffed and rolled — see recipes for Fish Stuffing which follow.

The smelt don't have to be skinned as the skin is very mild in flavor.

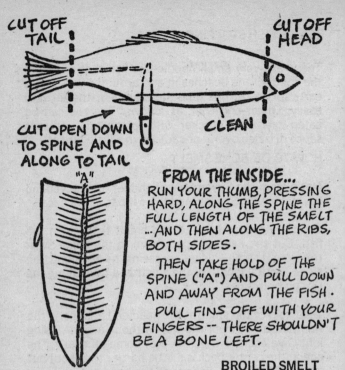

CUT OFF TAIL

CUT OFF HEAD

CUT OPEN DOWN TO SPINE AND ALONG TO TAIL

CLEAN

"A"

FROM THE INSIDE...

RUN YOUR THUMB, PRESSING HARD, ALONG THE SPINE THE FULL LENGTH OF THE SMELT ...AND THEN ALONG THE RIBS, BOTH SIDES.

THEN TAKE HOLD OF THE SPINE ("A") AND PULL DOWN AND AWAY FROM THE FISH.

PULL FINS OFF WITH YOUR FINGERS -- THERE SHOULDN'T BE A BONE LEFT.

BROILED SMELT

Dip them in a mixture of:
¼ cup of melted butter
1 tbsp of lemon juice and
a dash of salt then
Dip in **flour** and place on a broiler rack. Sprinkle with **salt** and broil for a few minutes until golden, turn and broil the other side until golden.
Serve with any of the seafood sauces.
Take bones out as illustrated on page 110 unless you are like my husband and eat bones and all.

DEEP FRIED SMELT IN PUFFY BATTER

Clean and dry **smelt** with paper towelling, dip in **flour** then deep fry using **Deep Fried Puffy Batter** recipe page 152 and fry until golden color.

JEAN'S FISH STUFFING

Melt **4 tbsp of margarine [¼ cup]** in the top of a double boiler.

Cut into small cubes **4 slices of white bread** and add them to the margarine.

Sprinkle **1 tsp of poultry seasoning** over bread

Add a **dash of salt** and

½ cup of chopped green onion and mix.

This is enough stuffing for 8 de-boned smelt.

GLADYS' FISH STUFFING

This recipe comes from Gladys of the Big Crab Seafood Stores.

Saute **¼ cup each chopped celery, fresh parsley** and **onion** in

2 tbsp of butter

Add **½ tsp of lemon pepper**

½ tsp thyme

Cut into small cubes **4 slices of white bread** and add them to the butter.

Drain a **10 oz. tin of whole tomatoes** well, chop and add to the bread. Drink the juice.

Add **¼ lb. of shrimp** and toss.

The above stuffings are tasty with salmon as well as any of the white fish. You can layer the fish and stuffing in a casserole instead of rolling the thin stuffed fillets.

OOLICHANS

Use Smelt Recipes above.

CLEANING AND COOKING CRABS

The time honored method of cooking crabs is to plunge them alive in boiling sea water and cook them for 15 minutes after water returns to a boil. This requires a large pot if you have a good catch.

Another method is becoming more popular and has many advantages. The crab is killed and cleaned **before** cooking so that only the meat and surrounding shell is cooked. This saves a great deal of space in the cooking pot. I have found that up to three times as many crabs can be cooked in this manner as compared to boiling them in the shell.

This method also cuts down some of the odor from cooking entrails and makes subsequent shelling of the meat less messy. As well, it prevents squeamish people from feeling like cannibals throwing missionaries into the pot. (Yes, it is true that crabs often squeal when dropped into boiling water.)

Commercial crab operations boil alive only the crabs they will sell fresh and whole. The retail customer often likes to buy the whole animal. It has an attractive color after cooking and the shell can be used as a decoration or even to hold the crab meat when serving.

Some customers also feel they are getting fresher crab if they buy it in the shell. This may be true if they buy it direct from a vendor with a cooking pot next to his stand. (This is the situation at colorful Fisherman's Wharf in San Francisco.) But if you buy crab in a supermarket or fish shop, both whole crab and the shelled meat are probably of equal freshness.

The other apparent advantage of buying whole crab is the lower price per pound. You must remember, however, that shell, entrails, and other inedible material make up more than half the total weight. You will also have the labor of picking the meat from the shell.

If you have caught your own crab, the clean first method is far more efficient. I learned this method originally from watching commercial crab pickers on the Oregon coast many years ago. I copied their style and recommended it in previous editions of this book.

In gathering information for this revised and expanded book, I discovered what seems to me an even faster and easier way to clean crabs. Roger

Reed and Pat Naduriak of Dennis' Shellfish in Victoria were kind enough to demonstrate this new method for me. Sometimes their hands moved almost too fast to follow but, with the aid of motion pictures, we were able to isolate the details of how they did it.

Prop up a shovel or other narrow edged tool to use as a striking surface. If you have a large barrel or garbage can, place the shovel, handle down, in the barrel. This will hold the sharp edge up vertically and will also catch the shell and entrails as they fall away when the crab is killed.

(SHOVEL)

Grasp the crab by the four back legs as shown in the diagram. Freshly caught crabs will be very lively and will fight back vigorously, so handle them like a porcupine makes love (. . . very carefully!) If you leave the crabs out of water under a wet sack, they will become lethargic after an hour or two and will be easier to handle. (Do not expose them to hot sun or drying wind or they will die quickly.)

1. Hold crab (facing away from you) with four rear legs in each hand...

Hold the crab an inch or two above the shovel's edge, then crack down sharply, striking the crab's narrow underflap against the shovel. This will break the crab into three pieces. The underside will split along the line of the flap and leave two sections, each containing four legs, a pincer claw, and a knot of body meat. The carapace or top shell will stick to the edge of the shovel or fall away into the barrel.

2.   **3.**

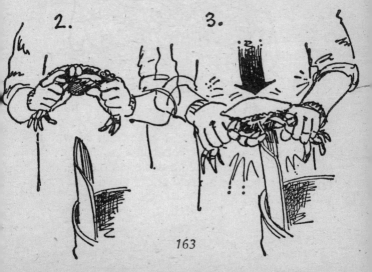

Some persons watching this procedure for the first time think it is cruel or inhumane, but this is not true. It kills the crab instantly and is better, in my opinion, than dropping the crab alive into . boiling water.

Clean away the bits of entrails still clinging to ·the body sections and the crab is ready for cooking.

Another effective way of cleaning the crab is with a knife or hatchet. Lay the crab on his back and place the knife or hatchet along the flap. Now strike the back of the knife with your fist or a mallet. This blow is a short punch or tapping action, firm enough to break through the undershell, but not enough to cut clear through the top shell or carapace.

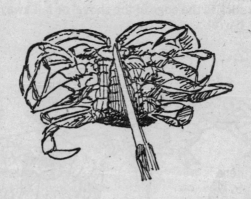

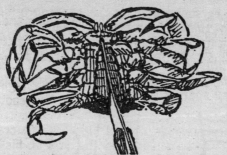

Now grasp one set of legs and twist them away from the shell, bringing the attached body meat with them. Hold the knife with the other hand to keep the crab shell in place. Then switch hands and twist away the other set of legs and body meat.

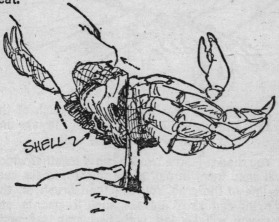

SHELL

If there is no shovel, suitable knife, or hatchet handy, you can use the method suggested in earlier editions of this book. It is quite satisfactory, but takes a bit more practice to become proficient at holding the crabs properly...

Grasp the crab by the upper leg joints and pull them back from the front face of his main shell. This will expose the front edge of the shell. Find a protruding object such as the edge of a table, stair, sharp rock, etc. and strike the front edge of the shell sharply against it.

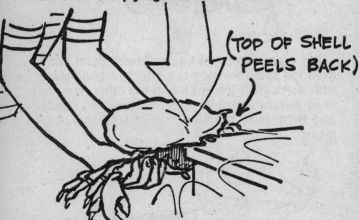

(TOP OF SHELL PEELS BACK)

You will find that the shell and much of the crab's entrails will peel away from the legs and body meat much like shelling a walnut.

You then twist the two leg joints together which will snap them in half along the front-back centerline of the crab. You can then brush off the clinging chunks of entrails, shell fragments, etc. and you will be left with two crab segments containing four legs and a claw connected to a large pyramid shaped knot of body meat encased in a honeycomb of thin translucent shell....

COOKING THE CRABMEAT

These segments can then be cooked in boiling salt water for 15 minutes. It is important to cook these segments as quickly as possible since raw crab meat deteriorates very quickly. It is not absolutely necessary to cook the crabs in sea water or even salt water, but the salt water adds flavor. Many persons even add a great deal of salt to sea water to enhance the flavor of the cooked crab meat.

Others feel it is better to cook the crab in fresh water. They feel this retains the completely natural crabmeat flavor. (I find this quite bland.) They also claim the meat is more tender. Some crabs are cooked less than 15 minutes in an attempt to keep the meat tender. This may help, but it is important that they be cooked at least 10 minutes to kill bacteria.

After cooking, the crabs should be soaked for a few minutes in cold water. This cools the shells, which otherwise would continue transmitting heat to the meat, overcooking it and causing it to be dry and tough.

Cooling the crabs immediately after cooking seems to help the meat pull free from the shell and makes subsequent cleaning easier.

CRACKING CRABS AND PICKING THE MEAT

Picking the meat out of the shell by hand is a long and tedious process involving nut crackers, pointed forks and other instruments to separate meat from the shell.

Commercial operators have evolved several methods to speed up the process. These techniques work on the principle that crab meat (or muscle) consists of fibers which run basically parallel to the long axis of the shells. If the ends of the shells can be opened up, the meat can be shaken or knocked out the opening.

The body meat is easiest to clean. It is encased only in a light, translucent shell which is quick to open. The whole body cavity section (for half a crab) can be pressed under the butt of your open hand, cracking the shell and opening up the segments of meat. Bits of shell on the edge of the body section can be cleaned away and the section is ready for cleaning.

PLACE LEG SEGMENT (LEGS & CLAW), BOTTOM-SIDE UP, ON A HARD SURFACE AND CRACK BODY MEAT SHELL WITH HEEL OF HAND...

The whole body segment can be cleaned at once or broken up into four segments. If it is cleaned whole, grasp the legs and strike the body end of the legs against the edge of a pan or bowl. This should be a short, shaking motion, and the crab meat should pop out of the body shell when it bumps the edge of the pan.

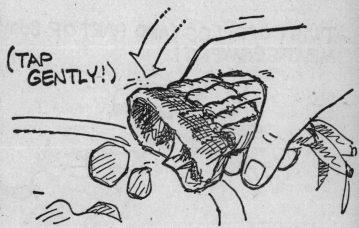

(TAP GENTLY!)

Do not use a swinging motion (like hammering a nail) or you are likely to have crabmeat all over the walls. The meat often comes loose, but doesn't quite fall out. If you move up vigorously for the next blow, the meat is very likely to fly out on the upswing.

KLONK!
WHIZ!
P'O!

Alternatively, break off each leg (with its attached cluster of meat and shell) and shake out the body meat. This may take slightly longer, but is easy to learn and very effective.

TWIST OFF LEG (AND PART OF BODY MEAT SEGMENT)...

TAP EACH LEG ON EDGE OF BOWL TO DISLODGE MEAT FROM BODY SEGMENT...

Cleaning the legs is done in a very similar manner. The body end of the leg shell is broken away and the lower joints are twisted off. (There is some meat in these joints, but commercial operations don't feel it is worth the trouble to get it out.)

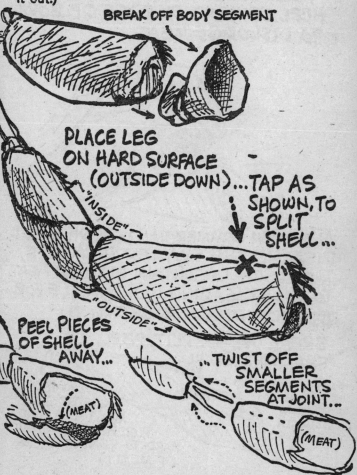

BREAK OFF BODY SEGMENT

PLACE LEG ON HARD SURFACE (OUTSIDE DOWN)...TAP AS SHOWN, TO SPLIT SHELL...

"INSIDE"

"OUTSIDE"

PEEL PIECES OF SHELL AWAY...

(MEAT)

...TWIST OFF SMALLER SEGMENTS AT JOINT...

(MEAT)

Hold the main leg segment (with the open end down) between your thumb and forefinger and bump the side of your hand against the pan. The leg meat should pop out in one delicious chunk.

HOLD SEGMENT AS SHOWN. TAP HEEL OF HAND ON EDGE OF BOWL TO DISLODGE MEAT.

ALTHOUGH COMMERCIAL OPERATIONS DISCARD THE SMALLER SEGMENTS, THEY USUALLY CONTAIN ENOUGH MEAT* TO MAKE CLEANING WORTHWHILE FOR THE INDIVIDUAL CRABBER...

BREAK OPEN, SPLIT, PEEL, SHAKE INTO BOWL...

*AN EXCEPTION IS THE SMALL, HIND LEG... NOT WORTH THE BOTHER!

(BREAK OFF, USE TIP SEGMENT AS A HANDY PICK FOR PRYING OUT HARD-TO-REMOVE PIECES OF MEAT!)

174

The last portion to be cleaned is the pincer claw. Its different shape requires another procedure. The triangular cross-section of the upper segment can be cleaned easily.

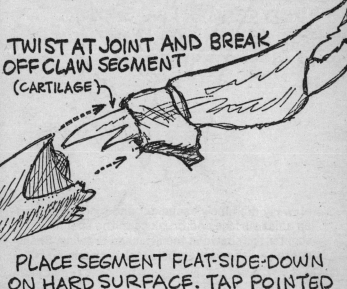

TWIST AT JOINT AND BREAK OFF CLAW SEGMENT

(CARTILAGE)

PLACE SEGMENT FLAT-SIDE-DOWN ON HARD SURFACE. TAP POINTED EDGE TO SPLIT SHELL...

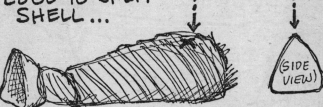

(SIDE VIEW)

PEEL AWAY END OF SHELL, SHAKE MEAT OUT, AS WITH LEG SEGMENTS.

Twist off the movable section of the pincer, pulling out the internal cartilage connected to it.

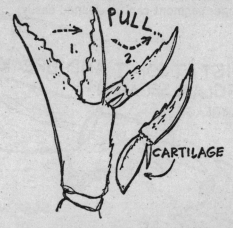

Now lay the "elbow" segment and pincer segment on a flat surface and break open the shell in each segment as shown in the attached drawing. Shake out the meat and the whole crab is cleaned.

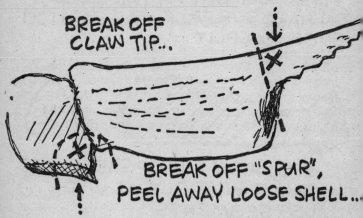

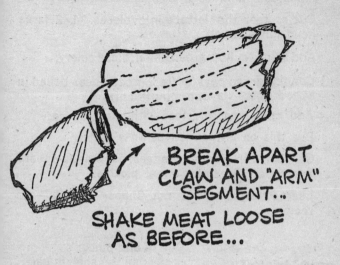

**BREAK APART
CLAW AND "ARM"
SEGMENT...
SHAKE MEAT LOOSE
AS BEFORE...**

Keep the meat chilled and well covered or wrapped to prevent it from drying out. Eat it as soon as possible. All seafood deteriorates quickly, but crabmeat goes downhill very fast.

Crabmeat can be frozen, but it tends to get rubbery, especially in a home freezer. Commercial freezing plants can flash freeze crabmeat, subjecting it to a high volume blast of very cold air. This frozen product is much better, but the texture still suffers in comparison with fresh crabmeat.

CRAB SALAD

Cut or tear the **lettuce** into pieces. (1/2 large head for 4 people.)

Add a little cut up **green onion, diced celery,**

Canned **green peas** (or fresh frozen peas boiled in salted water for one minute only).

Add **crab meat** and toss with **mayonnaise.**

Pile this on lettuce leaves on a platter.

Garnish with **Tomato wedges, asparagus spears, cucumber slices** and **sweet pickles.**

I serve this salad with hot **Cheese Biscuits** - see recipe.

CRAB COCKTAIL

Place shelled cooked **crab** in a small glass or dish and add a small amount of the following:

Mayonnaise mixed with a little **ketchup** or...

Salad dressing mixed with a little **ketchup** or...

Mock Tartar Sauce - see recipe.

A NO - NO! Don't drown the lovely subtle flavor of the crab by using a **hot** tomato sauce!

Crab can be stretched to go further by mixing it with steamed, baked or boiled cod that has been flaked.

CREAMED CRAB

Make the following sauce in a double boiler.

Melt **2 tbsp of margarine or butter** in the top.

Add **2 tbsp of flour,**

1/2 tsp of salt,

Pour in **1 cup of milk or cream,**

Add **2 tbsp of diced green onion** and

1 diced hard boiled egg,

Stir in **1 cup of shelled, cooked crab meat,**

Heat for two or three minutes and
Serve on **Toast** or on **rice.**

This amount serves 3 or 4 people.

CURRIED CRAB

Make the following curried sauce in a double boiler.

Melt **2 tbsp of margarine or butter** in the top,

Add **2 tbsp of flour,**

1/2 tsp of salt

1/2 tsp of curry powder and stir together (this amount makes a very mild dish.)

Pour in **1 cup of milk or cream,**

Add **2 tbsp of ketchup.**

Stir continuously until thickened then add shelled, cooked crab and heat for two or three minutes.

Serve on rice or over a piece of toast.

Boil **1/2 cup of long grain rice** in salted water for 15 minutes.

(It is not so apt to boil over if you put **1 tbsp of cooking oil** in the water).

Add **1/2 cup of frozen green peas** to the boiling rice water and cook for 1 minute only.

Drain and keep the rice and pea mixture hot in a casserole while you make the Crab Newberg.

Melt **2 tbsp of margarine or butter** in the top of a double boiler.

Add **1/8 tsp of Seafood Seasoning,**

1/4 tsp of salt,

1 cup of shelled, cooked crab meat (approximately 4 oz.).

Heat with lid on at medium heat.

If you won't be ready for the Newberg right away, turn the heat under the boiler to simmer.

Beat **2 egg yolks** in a bowl and add

1/2 cup of cream, canned or fresh.

Have **2 tbsp of medium sherry** on hand.

Five minutes before you are ready to serve
Stir the sherry into the crab then
Add the egg yolk and cream mixture and
Stir continuously until thickened.

Remove immediately from the heat the minute it thickens or it will separate. This won't hurt the flavour but it spoils the looks.
This amount serves 3 or 4 people.

Look for these books of outdoor exploration and discovery to help you get the most from B.C.'s great outdoors!

Available at your bookstore or sporting goods store — or you can order them from Heritage House Publishing Company on the convenient order form at the end of this book.

HOW TO CATCH SALMON — BASIC FUNDAMENTALS
by Charles White

This is the most popular salmon fishing book ever written! Here's the basic information you need for successful fishing: trolling patterns, rigging tackle, how to play and net your fish, downriggers — and where to find fish! Also included is valuable Fisheries Department information on the most productive lures, proper depths to fish and salmon habit patterns. This is *the* basic book on salmon fishing in the North Pacific with sales over 120,000. Illustrated throughout.

12th printing	176 pages	$5.95

HOW TO CATCH SALMON — ADVANCED TECHNIQUES
by Charles White

The most comprehensive salmon fishing book available! Over 250 pages crammed full with how-to tips and easy-to-follow diagrams to help you catch more salmon. Covers all popular methods — downrigger techniques, mooching, trolling with bait, tricks with spoons and plugs. You'll find tips for river mouth fishing, catching giant tyees, winter fishing, secrets of dodger and flasher fishing, Buzz Bombs, Deadly Dicks, Sneaks and other casting lures — and much more!

5th printing	256 pages	$8.95

HOW TO CATCH BOTTOMFISH
by Charles White

While salmon are the "glamour" fish, bottom-fish are tasty and easy to catch. This book shows how to catch cod, sole, perch, snapper, rockfish, and other bottomfish. Best tackle and rigs, baits, when and where to fish. Detailed step-by-step filleting diagrams.

Revised 5th printing   160 pages $4.95

HOW TO CATCH CRABS
by Captain Crabwelle

This book, revised to show the latest crabbing techniques, describes how to catch crabs with traps, scoops, and rings; where and when to set traps; the best baits to use. It includes a detailed description of an easier, improved method of cleaning, cooking and shelling the meat. It's a great book, crammed with everything you need to know about catching crabs.

Updated 11th printing   110 pages $4.95

HOW TO CATCH SHELLFISH
by Charles White

How, when and where to find and catch many forms of tasty shellfish: oysters, clams, shrimp, mussels, limpets. Easiest way to shuck oysters. Best equipment for clamming and shrimping. When not to eat certain shellfish. What to eat and what to discard. A delightful book of useful information. Well illustrated.

Updated 4th printing   144 pages $3.95

HOW TO CATCH STEELHEAD

This book by popular outdoors writer Alec Merriman contains helpful information for novice or expert. Information includes how to "read" the water, proper bait, techniques for fishing clear or murky water, and fly fish for steelhead. Many diagrams and illustrations.

5th printing   112 pages $3.95

HOW TO CATCH TROUT

Lee Straight is one of Western Canada's top outdoorsmen. Here he shares many secrets from his own experience and from experts with whom he has fished. Chapters include trolling, casting, ice fishing, best baits and lures, river and lake fishing methods — and much more.

8th printing   144 pages $4.95

HOW TO FISH WITH DODGERS AND FLASHERS

Joined by guest authors Lee Straight, Jack Gaunt and Bruce Colegrave, Jim Gilbert helps you catch more salmon. Find out when to use a dodger or a flasher, all about bait and lure hookups, best lure action, trolling speeds, leader lengths and more.

2nd printing   128 pages $3.95

DRIFT FISHING

Seven expert Pacific Coast fishermen help you become more productive using Perkin, Buzz-Bomb, Stingsilda, Deadly Dick, and herring. Whether you fish salmon, bottomfish or trout this book of illustrated techniques for mooching, casting and jigging can increase your catch.

Revised 3rd edition. 176 pages $5.95

HOW TO COOK YOUR CATCH
by Jean Challenger

Tells how to cook on board a boat, at a cabin or campsite. Shortcuts in preparing seafood for cooking, cleaning and filleting. Recipes and methods for preparing delicious meals using simple camp utensils. Special section on exotic seafoods. Illustrated.

8th printing 192 pages $4.95

BUCKTAILS AND HOOCHIES

Trolling bucktail flies is one of the most exciting methods of catching salmon, as well as being very productive. Hoochies have always been the favorite of commercial fishermen and expert Jack Gaunt tells sportsmen how to catch salmon with them.

3rd printing 112 pages $3.95

A CUTTHROAT COLLECTION

Until now little has been written about this popular quarry. This collection fills the void. Experts Bob Jones, Dave Stewart, David Elliott, Ron Nelson, John Massey, Ian Forbes and Karl Bruhn pool their knowledge and experience to unravel the mysteries surrounding this elusive fish.

94 pages $5.95

AN EXPLORER'S GUIDE TO THE MARINE PARKS OF B.C.
by Peter Chettleburgh

The definitive guide to B.C.'s marine parks. Includes anchorages and onshore facilities, trails, picnic areas and campsites. Profusely illustrated with color and black and white photos, maps and charts, this is essential reading for all yachtsmen and small boat campers.

200 pages $12.95

LIVING OFF THE SEA
by Charles White

Detailed techniques for catching crabs, prawn, shrimp, sole, cod and other bottomfish; oysters, clams and more. How to clean, fillet, shuck — in fact everything you need to know to enjoy the freshest seafood in the world. Black and white photos and lots of helpful diagrams.

Updated 2nd printing   128 pages $7.95

CHARLIE WHITE'S
101 SALMON FISHING SECRETS
by Charles White

Charlie shares more than a hundred of his special fishing secrets to help improve technique and increase your catch. No fisherman should pass this one up. Illustrated throughout with Nelson Dewey's distinctive cartoons and helpful diagrams.

Updated 3rd printing   144 pages $8.95

FLY FISH THE TROUT LAKES
with Jack Shaw

Professional outdoor writers describe the author as a man "who can come away regularly with a string when everyone else has been skunked." In this book, he shares over 40 years of studying, raising and photographing all forms of lake insects and the behaviour of fish to them. Written in an easy-to-follow style.

2nd printing   96 pages $7.95

SALMON FISHING BRITISH COLUMBIA:
Volume One — Vancouver Island

Vancouver Island is one of the world's best year-round salmon fishing areas. This comprehensive guide describes popular fishing holes with a map of each and data on gear, best time of year, most productive fishing methods and much more.

128 pages $9.95

LOWER MAINLAND BACKROADS

This best selling series is a complete guide to backroads from Vancouver to Clinton in the Southern Cariboo, and includes the Fraser Valley, Garibaldi, Lillooet and Bridge River Country. Well illustrated with photos and detailed route maps.

LOWER MAINLAND BACKROADS:
Volume 1
— Bridge River Country, Garibaldi to Lillooet
by Richard Thomas Wright

Revised edition of a best seller. This detailed guide to highways and byways includes route mileage, fishing holes, wildlife, history, maps and many photos.

168 pages $9.95

LOWER MAINLAND BACKROADS:
Volume 2
— The Fraser Valley
by Richard and Rochelle Wright

Detailed mile-by-mile backroads guide to the Fraser Valley and into the Coast Mountains. Includes information on fishing, history, campsites and much more, complete with maps and photos.

224 pages $2.95

LOWER MAINLAND BACKROADS:
Volume 3
— The Junction Country, Boston Bar to Clinton
by Richard Thomas Wright

A complete update of this best selling guide to the Interior Plateau country with its canoeing, fishing, gold panning, hunting, rockhounding and other outdoor activities. Detailed maps and many photos.

164 pages $9.95

OKANAGAN VALLEY

Guide to a valley famous for its beaches and blossoms; paved highways, wineries and colorful history; sunshine and — perhaps — a genial Okanagan Lake resident called Ogopogo. Includes descriptions of major lakes and backroads, Okanagan wineries which feature visitor tours, and all communities. Photos, maps, four-color covers.

128 pages $3.95

HISTORIC FRASER AND THOMPSON RIVER CANYONS

The Trans-Canada Highway from Vancouver to Kamloops offers scenery from mountains to sagebrush, wildlife from mountain goat to muskrat, vegetation from dogwood to cactus. Here is a mile-by-mile guide — including its colorful history. Black and white and color photos plus map.

128 pages $7.95

BACKROADS EXPLORER:
Thompson-Cariboo
by Murphy Shewchuk

This comprehensive guide to the backroads of the Thompson-South Cariboo region is packed with information: points of scenic and historical interest; recreational facilities; best fishing areas; campsites and accommodation. Many photos and easy-to-follow maps.

176 pages $9.95

THE DEWDNEY TRAIL: British Columbia's Highway 3 from Hope to Fort Steele.

Built in 1865 over 400 miles from the Coast Mountains to the Rockies, this route is now paved Highway 3. With over 100 photos, this complete route description includes wildlife, government campsites, communities and history.

160 pages $9.95

THE BEST OF B.C.'s HIKING TRAILS
by Bob Harris

Here are 20 great hikes from all around B.C. to suit hikers of all levels of ability. Each hike is accurately described and mapped and you'll find complete details of how to get there and what you can expect to find. Illustrated throughout with black-and-white photographs, this is essential reading for all hiking enthusiasts.

174 pages $9.95

FORT STEELE: Here History Lives
by Derryll White

From a thriving 1890s community that called itself "The Capital of the Kootenays," Fort Steele declined to a ghost town. But it was reprieved when the B.C. Government began a restoration program which now attracts some 300,000 visitors a year. In 50,000 words with over 100 historical and contemporary photos and four-color covers, here Fort Steele lives again.

160 pages $9.95

GREAT HUNTING ADVENTURES

Like many young boys, Henry Prante's imagination was stirred by tales of big-game hunting in the Canadian wilderness. Here he shares his experiences while hunting bear, deer, moose and other big-game species.

144 pages $7.95

B.C. PROVINCIAL POLICE STORIES: Mystery and Murder from the Files of Western Canada's First Lawmen

The B.C. Police force was born in 1858, the first lawmen in Western Canada. These two popular books relate some of their adventures. All cases are reconstructed from archives and police files by ex-Deputy Commissioner Cecil Clark who served the force for 35 years.

VOLUME 1   128 pages $8.95
VOLUME 2   144 pages $9.95

PIONEER DAYS IN BRITISH COLUMBIA

Every article in this best selling, four-volume series is true, many written or narrated by those who, 100 or more years ago, lived the experiences they relate. Each volume contains 160 pages, four-color covers, some 60,000 words and over 200 historical photos, many published for the first time.

VOLUME 1 $9.95   VOLUME 2 $9.95
VOLUME 3 $9.95   VOLUME 4 $9.95

BOOK ORDER FORM

Heritage House Publishing Company

BOX 1228, STN. A, SURREY, B.C. V3S 2B3

Please send me the following books:

COPIES	TITLE	EACH	TOTAL
.....	BACKROADS EXPLORER - Thompson/Cariboo	$ 9.95	.....
.....	B.C. PROVINCIAL POLICE STORIES	$ 8.95	.....
.....	B.C. PROVINCIAL POLICE STORIES - Vol 2	$ 9.95	.....
.....	BEST OF B.C.'S HIKING TRAILS	$ 9.95	.....
.....	BUCKTAILS AND HOOCHIES	$ 3.95	.....
.....	CHARLIE WHITE'S 101 FISHING SECRETS	$ 8.95	
.....	CUTTHROAT COLLECTION	$ 5.95	.....
.....	DEWDNEY TRAIL	$ 9.95	
.....	DRIFT FISHING	$ 5.95	
.....	EXPLORER'S GUIDE TO MARINE PARKS	$12.95	.....
.....	FLY FISH THE TROUT LAKES	$ 7.95	
.....	FORT STEELE: Here History Lives	$ 9.95	.....
.....	GREAT HUNTING ADVENTURES	$ 7.95	
.....	HISTORIC FRASER-THOMPSON CANYONS	$ 7.95	.....
.....	HOW TO CATCH BOTTOMFISH	$ 4.95	.....
.....	HOW TO CATCH CRABS	$ 4.95	.....
.....	HOW TO CATCH SALMON - Advanced	$ 8.95	.....
.....	HOW TO CATCH SALMON - Basic	$ 5.95	.....
.....	HOW TO CATCH SHELLFISH	$ 3.95	.....
.....	HOW TO CATCH STEELHEAD	$ 3.95	.....
.....	HOW TO CATCH TROUT	$ 4.95	.....
.....	HOW TO COOK YOUR CATCH	$ 4.95	.....
.....	HOW TO FISH WITH DODGERS AND FLASHERS	$ 3.95	.....
.....	LIVING OFF THE SEA	$ 7.95	.....

LOWER MAINLAND BACKROADS:

#1 - Bridge River Country	$ 9.95	
#2 - Fraser Valley	$ 2.95	
#3 - Junction Country-Boston Bar		
to Clinton	$ 9.95	
.. OKANAGAN VALLEY	$ 3.95	
.. PIONEER DAYS IN B.C. - Vol 1	$ 8.95	
.. PIONEER DAYS IN B.C. - Vol 2	$ 8.95	
.. PIONEER DAYS IN B.C. - Vol 3	$ 8.95	
.. PIONEER DAYS IN B.C. - Vol 4	$ 8.95	
.. SALMON FISHING B.C. - Vol 1, Van. Island	$ 9.95	

SUB-TOTAL $

Add $1.00 per book for postage and handling .....

TOTAL $

My cheque for $ . . . . is enclosed

HERITAGE HOUSE
PUBLISHING COMPANY LTD.
Box 1228, Station A
Surrey, B.C. V3S 2B3

NAME (PLEASE PRINT)

ADDRESS

CITY   PROVINCE   POSTAL CODE

ALL PRICES QUOTED ARE CURRENT AT TIME OF GOING TO PRESS.
AS BOOKS ARE REPRINTED, HOWEVER, PRICES MAY CHANGE.